If How-To's Were Enough

We Would All Be

Skinny, Rich, & Happy

Brian Klemmer

insight
PUBLISHING GROUP

Tulsa, Oklahoma

IF HOW-TO'S WERE ENOUGH WE WOULD ALL BE SKINNY, RICH, & HAPPY
© 2005 by Brian Klemmer

Published by Insight Publishing Group
8801 S. Yale, Suite 410
Tulsa, OK 74137
918-493-1718

Original Printing: 50,000
Revised Printing: 20,000

Unless otherwise noted, all Scripture quotations are taken from the Holy Bible: King James Version.

ISBN 1-932503-40-4
Library of Congress catalog card number: 2004112952

Printed in the United States of America

Praise from corporations for Brian Klemmer and this book

"We were so impressed with Brian's training that we offered it to everyone in our factory! The effects were visible and immediate. Many, many employees thanked us for this opportunity to improve their personal lives. This book provides unique insights into the culture necessary for success in any organization. It focuses on people and personal responsibility. I recommend this to anyone who wants to improve themselves or their organization. It is more than a must read. It is a must do!"
—**Mike Simmons, Vice President of Finance and Planning, The Fulton Group of Companies**

"We have used Brian for customer service training, sales training, and for a management retreat over the last two years. This effort has helped us turn concepts like 'partnership and teamwork' from words into action. This book now makes these principles available to everyone for producing results in their personal and professional life."
—**Jim MacDonald, President and CEO, F.F. MacDonald**

"This book is long overdue. Brian's training programs have been at the top of their class. The insights on fundamental life issues and personal communication as well as understanding the real meaning of commitment, self-responsibility, and relationships are what can make a business team excel or an individual achieve superior performance and happiness. This is truly one of the rare programs that have had a lasting and permanent impact on the participants and where positive improvements are measurable. Definitely an outstanding training experience! Many thanks to Brian as he has affected our lives in a most positive and memorable way."
—**Jim Kirkland, National Service Manager, American Suzuki Motor Company**

Quotes from the network marketing industry for Brian Klemmer and this book

"I have been in network marketing for the last 18 months. In the first 11 months, I was not able to sign up anyone into my business due to fear and lack of commitment. After reading *If How-To's Were Enough* and attending the Personal Mastery and Advanced Leadership seminars, I became one of the top three enrollers in the company and won an all-expense-paid trip!"

—**Kimberly, Mannatech**

"After reading *If How-To's Were Enough* and attending both the Champions Workshop and Personal Mastery seminars, I set a goal to become one of the top recruiters in the entire company and within three months was recognized as the #2 recruiter in the entire company."

—**Hal Fischer, Pre-Paid Legal**

"After reading *If How-To's Were Enough* and completing the Personal Mastery seminar, my income actually tripled, and I advanced three levels in my USANA business, all within a month!"

—**Gail Stolzenburg, USANA**

"The book, *If How-To's Were Enough*, and the Klemmer leadership seminars are exactly what I needed to breakthrough and earn my pink Cadillac."

—**Linda Raube, Mary Kay**

"I have given away and sold hundreds of these books. I was already a Presidential prior to reading *If How-To's Were Enough*. After reading this book and experiencing the Klemmer leadership series of seminars, I tripled my income in the first year and won #1 associate in 2002, was a top 20 business builder in 2003, and the results keep getting better."

—**Merri-Jo Hillaker, Mannatech**

"Brian Klemmer is THE BEST speaker I have heard. Now he has produced THE BEST book. I'm recommending that everyone in my downline read it."

—Tim Sales, Big Planet

"The chapter on the 3R's will significantly increase the quality of all your relationships as well as be a foundation for how to build your business relationships."

—Dany and Debby Martin, NDA

"The chapter on the Formula of Champions by itself is worth 1,000 times what someone will pay for this book! It is the single biggest insight to producing results I have seen."

—Mitch Huhem, Unicity

"Everyone wants to do well at their network marketing business. Many books tell you what to do. This book will take you from someone who merely works the business to be a business builder."

—Jordan Adler, Excel Telecommunications

"If you are looking to make a dramatic increase in the effectiveness of your prospecting and coaching of your downline, this is the book to read."

—Donna Larson Johnson, Arbonne

"This book goes way beyond normal motivation and how to do the business, and provides network marketers the missing keys to be tops in their business."

—Jarman Massie, Royal Body Care

"Brian Klemmer has keynoted at our convention and trained the key leaders in our team to success. Now he has captured the essence of his training in this book. It is a must read for anyone serious about their business."

—Orjan Saele, Seven

Contents

Acknowledgments

This book is dedicated to my parents, Ken and Alice Klemmer, who were everything a child could want in parents. My thanks to my wife, Roma, and our three children, Kelly, David, and Krystal, who have been God's biggest blessing to me as well as some of my best teachers of the material in this book.

Thanks to Mark Victor Hansen, best-selling coauthor of the *Chicken Soup for the Soul* series and John Gray, best selling author of *Men Are From Mars and Women Are From Venus*. Despite their mega-star status, they have continuously taken time to support me as well as believe in me over the years.

Thanks to Lance Giroux of Allied Ronin for not only introducing me to this work, but for being a great friend since 1968. Thanks to my mentor, Tom, who passed away in 1983 and was the vehicle for me learning most of this work. Thanks to Tony Giovanni and Brian Mast for their technical support in making this book a reality and never once complaining about any of my changes or demands.

Thanks to all of our clients who have believed in K&A and the many thousands of participants who, through their willingness to explore ways to be more successful and contribute to others, have given me hope.

Thanks, lastly, to all the people who have made K&A a career and dedicated their lives to building "leaders who will create a world that works for everyone with no one left out."

Introduction

Welcome to the journey of personal growth, called **Personal Mastery**. It is a journey that begins each day and never ends. It is an exciting exploration of how you play the game of life and how your choices create your results. It is a journey available to all . . . and yet chosen by few.

Today you got up, went through your morning rituals, and embarked on the tasks of the day. Whether your mission involved leading a company or caring for a small child, you were called on to make thousands of choices over the course of the day. Which of these choices cost you the results you truly wanted?

The path to **Personal Mastery** enables you to discover what is behind the choices that do not support *you creating* your desires and to discover what it is you really want. It enables you to make different choices, choices that support what you really want.

As you might imagine, the path is not always easy to follow. It takes courage and commitment. You have to care a great deal about your results to work through the discomfort that accompanies personal breakthrough and growth. Yet the rewards are incredible! Life is more fulfilling, less stressful, and more fun. You are able to achieve your goals and to invent or create new ones.

Sound exciting? *It is!*

The intent of this book is to help you become a master of the game of life, able to create success as you define it on your terms. I feel blessed and honored to have the opportunity to share with you what I have learned, with the help of many who went before me along the path to **Personal Mastery**.

I applaud your willingness to explore and to reexamine some of your fundamental beliefs about life: who you are, what you think life is, what success is, and what you believe is required to be successful in life.

To best take advantage of this book, read it with an open mind and follow these suggestions:

- **Take time with this book.** Digest and continually explore its meaning for you. You will achieve the fullest appreciation for this book if you savor it, rather than gulp it down. Ultimately, your success will be measured by how much your viewpoint or perspective has changed, not in how quickly you read this book.

- **Write in it.** When you relate to a line or story on these pages, write in the book. As you read it the first time, highlight ideas and actions that you find meaningful in one color. The next time you read the book, highlight what jumps out at you in a different color. This will allow you to add emotion and speed to the process of change.

- **Be consistent.** A garden is best watered a little bit at a time, on a consistent basis, rather than flooding it all at once. Set up a plan of daily reading for a month and then follow it.

- **Allow yourself to react**. It will not serve you well to simply agree or to disagree with what is written here. Your thinking will shift as you struggle to gain different perspectives or viewpoints. *To Think Is to Create* is the premise of this book. If you want to create new results in your life (a better marriage, more income, more self-confidence, a closer relationship with God, or some other important change), then that will require new thinking or a different perspective. My mentor taught me, **"There is no fairer way to gauge anything than by results. Often harsh, but always fair."** React to this book and allow this book to deepen your understanding of *To Think Is To Create*.

- **Apply it.** Involve yourself in life. As you will discover, this is not a head trip, but rather an active process. As you begin to apply your new thinking, you will get feedback from life. Reread the book several times and continually apply your changed perspective until you achieve the results you truly want.

CHAPTER 1

You do not make
99 percent of your deci-
sions. Your programs
make them for you, but
you think you are
choosing.

The Secret

Most people in their search to "be better" will look for some "how-to's" or special techniques to help them "improve."

If they want to be wealthy, they look for someone to teach them "how-to" get rich.

If they want a better marriage, they look for a "how-to" on love.

If they want to lose weight, they look for "how-to" weight reduction help.

If they want a better relationship with their Creator, they look for "how-to" guidance.

You name it; people want to know the "how-to" secrets. *Unfortunately, this does not work!* If "how-to's" were enough:

- one top salesperson could teach others how to sell, and all salespeople would become excellent salespeople.

- one good student could teach study skills, and all students would become great students.

■ one exceptional manager could teach other executives how to manage, and all executives would become brilliant managers.

If "how-to's" were enough, we would all be skinny, rich, and happy. The fact is, most people do not do what they are told to do, nor do they do what they know is good for them.

People behave according to fundamental beliefs or subconscious thinking. You do not make 99 percent of your decisions; your programs make them for you, even though you think you are choosing. Your subconscious, or belief system, makes the majority of your decisions.

This is the secret of the ages!

Would you like greater liberty in your life? Examine the way your beliefs affect you, and you will see what I mean. Liberty, in this sense, is the ability to go where you want, when you want, not when someone else says you can or can't. It is the ability to have what you want, when you want to have it, not when your pocketbook or bank balance says you can or can't.

> **Your subconscious, or belief system, makes the majority of your decisions.**

It is the ability to do what you want to do, when you want to do it. Most importantly, it is the ability to be who you want to be, when you want to be it.

Freedom is the ability to decide; liberty is the result of wise decisions.

If it is true that 99 percent of all our decisions are made for us, or that even a majority are made by our subconscious, then we are not making our own decisions and are therefore *NOT* free. We are, in fact, about as likely to achieve a state of liberty as we are to win the lottery.

Some decisions are conscious in that you are aware of the choice. However, the decisions you need to explore if you want to have greater liberty are those enacted by your subconscious. This is, of course, if you want to create the life you desire.

What kind of subconscious decisions are we talking about? All kinds of decisions, such as: how you communicate with your children, whether or not to buy this book, whether to find a job, start a business, or invest in stocks, whether or not you will show up on time for a meeting, and how you feel right now. There are countless decisions that you make subconsciously.

It's all in how you look at it

Imagine that I was born wearing a pair of dark green sunglasses. A ridiculous sight, I agree, but let's say I've had these sunglasses on for my entire life and am now looking at the paper on which these words are printed. I would claim the paper is green.

If you tried to tell me it was white, I would tell you that you were wrong, that you didn't know what you were talking about. I might even say you should have *your*

eyes examined. It wouldn't matter to me how persistent you were, because I couldn't see white even if I wanted to. In short, there would be no hope of me actually seeing white while the glasses were on.

However, if I learned about sunglasses and I started looking for sunglasses, I might discover that I was wearing sunglasses. If I took them off, I would be able to see what I could not previously see—the color of the paper. In a second, I would have a revelation.

A simplistic example, but our lives are often like this. Someone tells us that we can make more money, get a job done in half the time, or work out a relationship problem. Even though we want to achieve a particular result, we have a hard time believing it is even possible.

Robert Kiyosaki, author of the best-selling book, *Rich Dad, Poor Dad*, tells people they can be multimillionaires. He knows they can. He went from being homeless to being a millionaire in less than five years, *but most people who listen to him cannot see that possibility in their circumstances*.

> **You cannot see solutions if your sunglasses will not allow you to.**

A good friend and client of mine, Peggy Long, is an extremely successful individual in a network marketing company. She reads people quickly and accurately and knows almost immediately if they have what it takes to be financially independent. Unfortunately, these individuals may not achieve financial independence even if they want to—if they cannot see what Peggy sees.

The key is for the individual to look for the sunglasses that are preventing them from seeing the solutions they already want.

What do you see?

What is the key to seeing your potential? You have to find and remove the sunglasses that prevent you from seeing the solutions you want. This is why "success" cannot be taught. You must experientially (not intellectually) begin to "see" life and yourself differently.

Let's look at this principle another way. Imagine that you live in Dallas, Texas and you hire me to speak to your company. You send me a map and instructions of how to get to your office. However, the map I receive is one for Chicago, but I don't know that because it says "Dallas." When I land at the airport, get to my rental car, and try to find your office, what happens? I get lost, confused, and frustrated. (The way many people feel as they try to progress.)

The names on the map do not align with your instructions, and I can't find the right streets. I call you on my cell phone and explain that the directions don't seem to fit. If you have a belief that the way to get ahead is to work harder, you will tell me, "You are not trying hard enough!"

At this point, I begin driving faster and search every street. I am working harder! Eventually, after two speeding tickets and a flat tire, I'm almost out of gas. Still lost, I call you again to vent my frustration.

You hear me out, and then if you had a belief that attitude is the key, you would tell me, "I can tell the problem. You have a bad attitude. The height of your altitude depends on your attitude." You are able to calm me down and tell me to read a positive thinking book.

Well, I'm teachable and I've done speed-reading courses, so I pull over and read a positive thinking book. When I start driving again, what happens? I'm just as lost as I was, I'm still about to run out of gas, the two speeding tickets are still in my pocket . . . only now I don't care because I have a positive attitude!

In terms of solving the problem—getting to your office— I still haven't made it. All along, the problem has been the fact that I had the wrong map and didn't know it. The problem was not my attitude or how hard I worked.

What if your map is wrong? *What if the map you are using, the one that tells you who you are, is incorrect?* Or maybe the map that tells you what commitment is? Or what responsibility is? With the wrong map, your hard work and positive attitude will not get you much closer to your dreams.

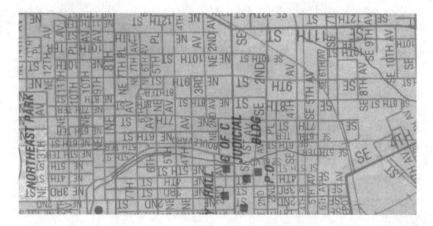

Many of you may honestly believe you have the right maps, but do you? If you are not getting the results you want in a particular area, then you do not have the right map. This does not mean there is anything wrong with you. You just need to find the right map.

Let's assume you had great parents. You have a map of good parenting. It's not just a theory, because you have experienced good parents, but there is a problem. The world has changed since you were a child. Years ago, chewing gum was the number one infraction in school. Today, smoking a joint, doing a line of crack, or getting a girl pregnant in school are very real concerns.

Or perhaps only one of your parents worked outside the home, but both you and your spouse work outside the home today.

The world has changed, so the map that worked for your parents will not work for you in every scenario in today's changed world. Times have changed . . . and old maps are ineffective.

Is your "life map" as outdated as the maps in your glove box?

In addition to maps being out of date, every person is different, so simply copying or modeling someone else's success doesn't always work. You are different and you are probably in a different situation, *which means you need a different map!*

One of the most exciting parts about all of this is how long it takes to take a set of sunglasses off: *seconds!*

Major advancements in your life can occur quickly. It does not have to take a long time. In our **Personal**

Mastery weekend seminar, I have seen thousands of what appear to be miracles occur in incomes, relationships, and health as a result of just a weekend of work. A weekend of finding sunglasses and taking them off.

The map to self-realization

One of the most important maps (really it involves several maps) is "Who are you." What you think you are often is more important than who you really are.

The beginning step in exploring this question requires you to think of yourself as a peanut M&M—the candy-coated chocolate with a nut in the middle. The color coating on the outside is your behavior, the white layers of candy that come next are your feelings, the chocolate is your subconscious thinking or programs, and the inner most part—the nut—is you.

Let's look closer at this simple model.

Are you your behavior?

I would say you are not. Some people are programmed to believe that they are their behavior. Say a parent catches a child stealing a cookie and says, "You are a bad boy." The child could believe this: "I did something bad, they say I am bad, therefore I must be bad."

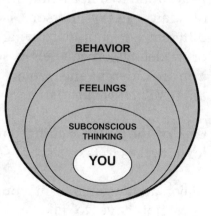

The child's subconscious map stated, "You are your behavior."

The problem with this viewpoint is simple. When you behave well, your self-esteem goes up, but when you behave badly or achieve poor results, your self-esteem goes down. Your self-esteem goes up and down like a yo-yo!

In reality, your behavior is much like a jacket in that it's not you. You wear it, but it isn't you. It doesn't comprise who you are. With this understanding, your self-esteem can remain high no matter what the circumstances.

Are you your feelings?

Again, I would suggest that you are not. If your behavior is your jacket, then feelings are your shirt or blouse. Your behavior and feelings do affect each other, but that doesn't mean that you are either of them.

Suppose two friends, Suzanne and Sarah, love to sing Karaoke on Wednesday nights. Let's say Suzanne has a bad day at work and Sarah calls Wednesday afternoon to see if Suzanne wants to sing Karaoke. Suzanne would probably say, "No, I don't feel like it." Her negative feelings determined her behavior. If Sarah insists and they go sing Karaoke, even though Suzanne really didn't "feel" like it, how does Suzanne feel after singing? Much better, right?

> Change comes in two flavors: *short-term and long-term.* Choose the one you want.

Suzanne changed how she behaved, and therefore changed how she felt.

If you do not feel the way you want to feel, *then change your behavior.* Or, if someone tells you, "You need to change your attitude," *then change your behavior*. Go for a walk, sing a song, jump up and down. *Do something different!* Your change in behavior will bring about the change in feelings and attitude that you want.

Changing your behavior to change your feelings or attitude can work, but only temporarily. This is why positive, pep-rally motivational seminars don't produce lasting results. They can't! This "outside-in" change is easy, but always shortlived because your subconscious thinking is making 99 percent of your decisions.

This does not mean temporary change is not important. Sometimes a "quick fix" can be useful. If you have had an argument at home and are on your way to an important sales meeting, jump up and down and yell, "I'm excited!" It may seem foolish, but you will feel better, and if you feel better, you will make better decisions, be more effective, and make more sales. However, just know it won't last.

What determines your behavior?

What truly determines your behavior and how you feel? I would say that 99 percent of the time it is your subconscious thinking.

For long-term change, look for your sunglasses, your maps, or your subconscious beliefs. They prevent you from seeing the solutions you want and achieving your dreams. Once you see white, you can never go back to believing that white does not exist. It is a revelation!

I have a plaque that a friend gave me years ago. It looks like a bunch of matchsticks on a board. At least that's what I saw. My friend laughed and asked me, "Don't you see it?"

It looked like a bunch of matchsticks to me. Then he said, "If you look at it properly, you will see that the sticks spell J-E-S-U-S."

Sure enough, once I *knew what I was looking for*, I saw it clearly. Now when I look at the plaque, I cannot help but see J-E-S-U-S.

The same thing happens when you start to see through different sunglasses. Once you have pierced the veil of darkness, you will see the light. You will begin to see everything differently.

CHAPTER #2

"On this rock I stand and
the whole world can
adjust to me."
– William Penn Patrick

RESULTS:
The Formula of Champions

Once upon a time, the story goes, there was a young boy named Aladdin. As he was kicking up the sand on a beach, he stubbed his toe on an old lamp. It looked intriguing, so he took it home. He spent hours chipping away clods of sand and then began to rub the lamp with a soft cloth to buff the metal. Suddenly a genie appeared and said to him, "Your wish is my command!"

Aladdin was stunned and decided to test the genie. He began by asking for a Big Mac hamburger. Puff! He received a Big Mac. Amazed, he asked for something larger: a camel. Puff! A camel appeared.

Excited, he asked for all the normal material things you might expect: a house, clothes, and money. Then Aladdin left his lamp on a shelf in his room and went on a cruise around the world.

While he was gone, one of the servants in Aladdin's household did some cleaning. The servant found what looked like an old lamp on the shelf where Aladdin left it. A merchant in the street below was yelling out, "Lamps for sale! Lamps for sale!" Without knowing the value of the lamp, the servant traded it for a new one.

When Aladdin returned from the cruise, he went looking for his magic lamp. When he couldn't find it, Aladdin panicked! He called his staff and asked if anyone had seen the old lamp. The servant proudly told him of the trade and showed him the new lamp.

Aladdin fell to his knees and wailed uncontrollably. He vowed that he would spend the rest of his life looking for that lamp, and that when he found it, he would never again let it out of his sight.

He spent the next ten years searching for the lamp and when he finally found the magic lamp for sale in a small shop, he was destitute. Since he could not afford the lamp, he offered to work for one year to buy it. The new owner, unaware of the lamp's value, agreed.

After a year of sweeping floors, closing up shop, and doing whatever chores the owner requested, Aladdin received his payment—the lamp. The lamp never again left Aladdin's sight and he always protected it, even at great expense.

Your Aladdin's lamp

Would you be willing to spend a year, tremendous energy, and perhaps thousands of dollars to have your own Aladdin's lamp?

I am about to share with you a formula that is just like Aladdin's lamp.

How badly do you want it? How hard would you work to keep it? Would you spend thousands of dollars? Would you go to a dozen seminars? Would you spend three years working to understand it?

Then suppose the formula that I am talking about could produce for you anything that you wanted. You would be excited, wouldn't you?

The most powerful formula I know—*The Formula of Champions*—has been used by Olympic athletes, Fortune 500 company executives, best-selling authors, world-renowned scientists, and master musicians, to name a few. *The challenge for you is to understand and apply the Formula of Champions.*

Personally, I would not accept any amount of money to surrender this formula. I have used it to:

- **raise millions of dollars for a cause I believed in, even though I had no experience raising large sums of money!**

- **buy houses when I had no money!**

- **bring into my life my beautiful wife and to create our fulfilling relationship (before I applied the formula, I was thirty-four years old, single, never married, and believed marriage was not possible for me)!**

I say these things not to brag, but to tell you how powerful the Formula of Champions really is! I do it to give you hope.

If you had a recipe for great chocolate chip cookies, you wouldn't have to have a great personality or a higher education to produce great cookies. You would simply need to follow the formula—the recipe.

So it is with the Formula of Champions. Here it is:

INTENTION + MECHANISM = RESULT

If you are anything like I was, you are saying to yourself, "So what? That doesn't seem so special."

At this moment, however, the Formula is only information in your conscious mind. For it to have the power of Aladdin's lamp, you must experience it. You must make the Formula part of your subconscious thinking (heart) by digesting it, applying it, and wrestling with it on a daily basis. Because, as Proverbs 23:7 states, *"For as he thinketh in his heart, so is he."*

> **The challenge for you is to *understand* and *apply* the Formula of Champions.**

Let's begin that process by defining each word in the formula:

INTENTION
According to the dictionary, intention is A) determination to act in a certain way and B) purpose, aim, end.

Intention is not merely willpower, for willpower comes from the conscious mind. Intention is a state of knowingness that comes from a deeper level (covered in chapter 5). It is deep clarity, with intensity. It is focus, certainty, and commitment.

MECHANISM
Mechanism is A) a piece of machinery and B) a process or technique for achieving a result.

A mechanism is simply a vehicle or way to accomplish something. It is the "how-to."

RESULT
Result is A) something that happens and B) effect, consequence.

To sum all three words together, *result is what you have after combining intention and mechanism.*

Does intention = result?

What if your intention always equaled your result? Wouldn't that be marvelous? You intend to get rich; you get rich. You intend to have a peaceful home; you have a peaceful home.

I believe that intention DOES equal result! **The problem is in differen-tiating what you want from your true intention.**

Before you argue, look at your hand. Let's call the palm of your hand "the front" and the other side "the back." Suppose you asked me for the front of my hand. I take out a knife and slice off the front of my hand.

But what remains? I still have a front and a back.

No matter how many times you ask for the front of my hand, I will always have a front AND a back. In fact, I cannot have a front without a back. You can tell them apart, but they are inseparable. Where one is, so is the other.

The front of your hand is intention; the back of your hand is result. You can use the Formula retroactively to look at the past and see what your "real" intentions were. You can also use it proactively to create the future results you want.

Let's say you had set a goal of earning $100,000 in a year and you only earned $70,000 last year. If we use the Formula to examine your result, we discover that $100,000 was not your real intention. That is not to say you didn't want to earn $100,000. You did, but your so-called intention was more like a want or an idle wish. It was not your deepest, most focused commitment. It was not your *true intention*.

Intention = Result

Perhaps, to reach your financial goal, you were unwilling to do something that might have made you look ridiculous or seem pushy. The result was a lost sale and you did not earn $100,000.

In other words, instead of making $100,000, you fulfilled that deeper, more focused desire—to earn more income as long as you did not look foolish or seem pushy. So, your *true intention*, was to not look pushy and was different than what you said you wanted.

Intention did equal the result.

Telling someone is not intention

If you have school-age children, for example, telling them to study in no way makes it their intention to study.

Or look at corporations. If they have quotas, they are constantly telling employees what to do and how to reach the required quotas, but just because the corporation wants something and tells the employees how to do it does not mean the employees intend, much less want, to meet those quotas.

Often, companies will hire Klemmer & Associates because they are frustrated. "We told our employees what to do in the form of quotas, but they are not reaching our goals." We have to explain that you cannot create an intention for people simply by telling them what to do or how to do it. They may pursue the goal out of compliance and lack commitment, while their *true intentions* are to be comfortable, not look good, not be rejected, or not to accomplish the goal.

You don't even know if people's *true intentions* are what they say they are. *True intentions* are often hidden—even from the very person declaring the intention!

In our **Personal Mastery** seminars, people tell us it is their intention to be financially independent when it is not their intention to be financially independent. We know this because they are not taking risks. They *want* to be wealthy. They have a *wish* to be wealthy. That is different than their *true intention*.

> **Telling people what to do does not make it their intention.**

We have couples who say that their intention is to have a happy marriage, and yet each person in the partnership is constantly trying to prove the other one wrong. It is their *true intention* to be right, not happy. They may *want* a happy marriage, but that is not their *true intention*.

Have you ever heard: "The road to hell is paved with good intentions." They were defining "intention" differently, more as a wish or a want. *True intentions* are much deeper, stronger, and more focused. Remember, "true intent" is your deepest commitment.

You can tell people's *true intentions* by the results they achieve, because intentions and results are always one and the same. Just as you cannot have a front of a hand without a back, you cannot have an intention without a corresponding result.

Did you set a New Year's resolution? Did you break it? If so, this formula says that keeping the resolution was not your *true intention*. Your *true intention* was something else. Perhaps it was to be right about why you can't keep your New Year's resolutions. Perhaps it was to be comfortable without challenging yourself.

What happens when the intent is clear

Imagine you are on one side of a room, and I tell you to cross the room one hundred times. It sounds easy enough to do, but there is a catch. Each time you cross the room you must use a different "mechanism." Perhaps you walk across the room and crawl back. Then you swim across and hop back. The walking, swimming, crawling, and hopping are all mechanisms.

After four trips across, perhaps you draw a blank. Only ninety-six more trips remain, yet you can't think of another way to cross the room! At that point, suppose I offer you a $100 bill if you come up with a new idea in fifteen seconds! An idea will come to you, seemingly, right out of the blue. However, it is not out of the blue.

A scientifically proven process has taken place. *When the intent is clear, a mechanism will appear.* In essence, you have told yourself, "Come up with a mechanism and come up with it now!"

Guess what happens! Your subconscious mind responds with a new mechanism.

If your *true intention* is to not look foolish, you may or may not make it across the room. If your *true intention* is to cross the room, then you will come up with a new idea. Your *true intention* won out!

When the intent is clear, a mechanism will appear.

Why do new ideas suddenly come to you? Maybe it's peer pressure, the desire to look good, your competitive nature, or some other reason. Regardless, *when the intent is clear, a mechanism will appear.*

This is a multimillion dollar concept!

You **do not** have to know **what** to do (the mechanism), but you **do** need an incredibly clear and intense intent, because intention comes before the mechanism and creates the mechanism.

I can tell you to cross the room one hundred times, and you may say you want to cross the room one hundred times, but the mechanism will not appear until it is your intention to do so.

When John F. Kennedy declared that America was going to put a man on the moon by the end of the 1960s, most people thought it was impossible because the science to do so, the mechanism, did not exist. But Kennedy's intention created the science or mechanism.

There are many other intention-before-mechanism examples, but most people wear sunglasses that are mechanism-oriented. They do not want to commit to a goal UNTIL they have the how-to mechanism in hand. *They have it backwards!*

> **After seeing hundreds of people cross the room with a different mechanism, it is easy to realize there are an infinite number of mechanisms for any one intention!**

People also wear sunglasses that limit the number of mechanisms they can use to accomplish goals. *These are sunglasses of scarcity.* They want to buy a house and they think there are only one or two ways to do so, such as put 20 percent down and borrow the other 80 percent.

When this mechanism doesn't work for them, they give up. If they can think of a second method, they might try again. If they happen to try the second time and fail, then they surrender and quit.

That is why I have people in our **Personal Mastery** seminars actually cross the room until they get stuck—so they can experience how the subconscious mind produces mechanisms. I want them to know experientially that if they raise the intensity level of their intention high enough, the "missing" mechanism will make itself plain.

Also, after seeing hundreds of people cross the room with a different mechanism, they realize there are an infinite number of mechanisms for any one intention! There are an infinite number of ways or mechanisms to communicate with a child, to buy a house, etc.

How to intensify your intention

You have conflicting intentions. You want to lose weight but you don't want to be disciplined. You want an intimate relationship but you don't want to be rejected.

The bigger intention is your *true intention*, and it always wins. The game becomes making what you want your *true intention* by raising its intensity higher than any conflicting intention. The bigger intention always wins.

Did you catch that? The key is to identify the conflicting intentions and then overcome them by intensifying your *true intentions*. Here are three ways to intensify an intention:

1. **Commit aloud to a friend who believes in you.** If you promise to exercise with a friend, you are more likely to do so. Why is this? Because you intensify your intention to exercise by making a promise so that your need to look good by keeping your promise overcomes your laziness or other conflicting intentions. You want to learn to commit

when you have no idea what to do. Making the promise creates the mechanism.

2. **Put your finances at risk.** Imagine that you want to buy a house in ninety days. Now, write a check for $10,000 payable to a charity. Tell a friend, "If I do not purchase a house in ninety days, donate this money to the charity." Would your intention, desire, and commitment to buy a house increase? I suspect it would. And you would be open to more new and previously unrecognized mechanisms.

3. **Visualize.** Athletes, religious leaders and scientists all urge people to use structured visualization to achieve their goals. If you doubt this, go shopping for a new car. Invariably, the sales representative will ask you, "Can you *see* yourself driving this automobile?"

    If you reply, "No, I can't," the sales rep will back away or show you a different car because all car salespeople know that you will give up on your goal of buying a new car if just one bank turns you down for a loan.

    However, if you reply, "Yes! I can see myself driving this car, but I can't afford it," see what happens. A good sales person will respond with, "Get in." If your subconscious absolutely has to have the car, after the test drive, you will find a mechanism to buy the car. You will change your work ethic or your job, if that's what it takes. Your elevated intention will produce a mechanism, seemingly from nothing!

    The average person won't even look at a new car until the mechanism is in place. They have the formula backwards.

Average people are average because of how they think, not because of their education, who they know, where they were born, their age, or any other external factor.

Successful people think and create. They know that *to think is to create.* If you do not think like a successful person, you will have difficulty producing success. We are not talking about adopting the personality of a successful person, but their subconscious thinking or belief, such as the Formula of Champions.

To reach your goal, to create the result you want, you have to examine and change your subconscious thinking—your fundamental beliefs about reality.

When your intent is clear, the mechanism will appear.

To learn more about this exciting and important topic, visit our Web site (www.klemmer.com) for a "Champion's Workshop" near you.

CHAPTER 3

Anger is a person's last
desperate attempt to avoid
responsibility and blame
the situation on someone
or something else.

The Key to Relationships

A small boy and girl were building a sand castle on the beach. They spent hours building towers, walls, and a moat. As they were building, the tide crept slowly in. Suddenly, a big wave wiped it all away.

An adult nearby felt sorry for them because of all the work they had put into building the castle, until the two children held hands and ran off together, laughing as they scampered down the beach.

It was then that the adult realized a simple truth: it is fun building empires, but the lasting fun is in having friends you can continue to laugh with and be with long after all that you have spent your life building has washed away.

Relationships are the key

Relationships are the key to making almost anything happen. They are the foundation to the quality of our lives and to the results we get.

Look around at anything manmade. Consider something small, like the salt and peppershakers on your table. How many people do you suppose it took to get those shakers to your table? There were people in manufacturing, as well as those in packaging and shipping. Supervisors and secretaries answered phones, salespeople sold the product to stores, and truck drivers delivered. There were those who invested in the company, and on and on. All these people were working in relation to each other with one goal in mind—to get those shakers to your table.

Are you beginning to see the interconnectedness in life and the importance of mastering relationships? Being "people smart" can make up for a lack of knowledge in many other areas.

The "3R's" that hold us back

A destructive thought process prevents successful professional and personal relationships, ruins communication, destroys teamwork, causes divorce, creates physical illness, causes loneliness, and costs businesses billions of dollars each year. This particular negative thought process is as damaging as drinking poison.

You might be wondering why we are even discussing a negative thought process? The reason is simple: *you think this way.*

Every human being I have ever met, without exception, has experienced this self-destructive thought process. This way of thinking was formed at a very tender age and is now ingrained in most of us.

> **Who has a negative thought process?**
> **You do!**

Why would intelligent people practice such a negative thought process? Perhaps it is because we do not connect a thought process directly to the damage it can cause. For example, if you touch a hot stove today, but the burn doesn't show up for six months, you might touch it frequently because you don't realize the connection.

No one changes their way of being until they see the high cost or price of their behavior. Most of the time, instead of changing, we remain in denial. We don't tell the truth about the cost or price because it hurts to accept it. Open up to the true hurt this thought process causes you and others and you will reduce or eliminate it from your life. That is why overcoming this poisonous thought process is the key to achieving high quality, positive, constructive relationships.

> We change *ONLY* when we see the high cost or price of our behavior.

The destructive thought process I'm referring to includes **resentment**, **resistance**, and **revenge**. I call it the "3R's." Let's take a closer look at each "R" individually.

RESENTMENT

Resentment is any negative emotional reaction to what we think has been said or done. Common emotions include: anger, frustration, sadness, jealousy, and hate.

On a day-to-day basis, you may experience resentment:

- when your spouse squeezes the toothpaste tube in the middle,

- when your child talks back to you,

- when someone cuts you off in traffic,

- when the person ahead of you at the grocery store has twenty items in the express lane,

- when the company you work for restructures, and you lose your job,

- when someone you love dies at the hands of a drunk driver,

- and countless other ways!

Resentment is a natural part of life. In fact, if you do not experience resentment, you are emotionally numb or dead. Thousands of people starve to death every day. How can you not feel resentment, unless you are emotionally numb?

Even if you are numb or masking your feelings, you still experience resentment. It is still there and it still hurts. Many people choose to live in a world of indifference for this very reason.

Others have been told that resentment is inherently bad, so they think there is something wrong with them when they experience resentment. The truth is, resentment occurs in any relationship, no matter how good it is. It occurs on the job, no matter how good the company you work for is.

The real question is: *How will you handle resentment?* The way you handle resentment can turn your life around. It can also destroy you if it leads you to RESISTANCE.

RESISTANCE
Resistance is the cutting off of communication or putting up a wall.

We resist in many ways. For example, if a married couple has an argument (resentment), and the husband rolls over to one side of the bed, and the wife turns the other way, you have resistance. They are not talking to each other. They are resisting each other. Communication has been cut off. Prices are being paid.

However, refusing to talk is only one of the ways to resist. People who procrastinate or feel confused are resisting something. When a manager hides behind a closed office door rather than face disgruntled employees, the manager is building a physical separation or a wall of resistance. When we have a problem at home and we bury ourselves in our work, or the television, or sleep, or food, we are resisting. When we insist on always "being right," that lack of openness is resistance.

Resist List		
What I resist	The ways I resist	The prices for resisting

I suggest that you make a list of what you resist, the ways you resist, and the prices that you and others are paying.

For example:

■ **What I'm resisting:** communicating with a loved one.

■ **The ways I'm resisting:** procrastinating and changing topics.

■ **The prices I (and others!) am paying:** lack of intimacy, loneliness, lack of friendship, feelings of guilt, embarrassment, etc.

Most often, we resist something in order to stay in or gain control. Here begins a fundamental problem in our belief systems and how we see reality.

In our **Personal Mastery** seminars, I ask a participant to sit facing me in a chair. What this participant does is a perfect example of our ingrained resistance nature. As to be expected, most participants do the same thing.

I ask these participants to raise their arms and hands, palms facing me. I push on their hands, and they push back, resist, and tip over in the chair.

This exercise raises two very important questions:

Question #1: Why do they push back? The answer is, they believe they must push back to stay in control. As we have already mentioned, we do not decide 99 percent of all our behavior. Our subconscious thinking decides for us. Our set of sunglasses or point of view makes the decision.

In this case, most people have been programmed to believe, "If someone pushes on you, you must push back to survive." As a result, the participants push back "to survive." The problem is, they don't survive. The chair tips over (we have someone there to catch them).

Think of a time when a boss, employee, parent, child, or lover pushed on you. Perhaps they tried emotionally or factually to prove you wrong. Did you push back? Did you argue with them to try and prove them wrong?

Question #2: Do you realize that your belief is false? This is critical. You think it is necessary to push back to survive, to gain control, and to not be taken advantage of, yet what happened in the chair demonstration? The person pushing back actually lost control! They even fell over backwards if they kept resisting. This clearly demonstrates that *when you resist, you lose control.*

Why do children make parents mad? Because children want to gain control. How are children five minutes after an argument? They are fine. How are you five hours later? Is steam still coming out your ears? If so, that is because you are resisting reality. A little voice inside your

What you resist . . . persists.

head is saying, "It shouldn't be this way." But it is! Resistance occurs when people say to themselves, "It shouldn't be this way."

What you resist persists. Read that again. *What you resist persists.* It prolongs what you don't want. That being the case, what are you resisting? Perhaps it is your weight, being alone, using the Internet, making cold calls, a certain aspect of your job, doing paperwork, or going back to school?

Who are you resisting? Your spouse, child, boss, or friend?

What price are you paying for your resistance? What prices are others paying for your resistance? What price is your business or your company paying?

No one changes until they see that the price they and others are paying is higher than the price they want to pay. I am not recommending that you become a doormat, that you let yourself be taken advantage of, or that you become passive.

You might be wondering, "How can I cease resisting and not be taken advantage of?" Good question, and I'll answer that with an analogy from Martial Arts. Most Martial Arts students learn not to resist. They are taught to redirect the attacking force—to use that force to throw the attacker on the ground. In fact, in the martial art Aikido, you protect yourself *and* the attacker. There is no separation between the one attacking and the one being attacked.

We conduct sales seminars using this metaphor to create top performers and teach that if you resist objections, you become a nonperformer. Instead, if you relate to objections as though they are friends, helping you close the sale, then you become a top performer.

One of my students many years ago was a gentleman named Bob Tourtelot. He was and still is a successful attorney. He was skeptical at first about this perspective. He had gained much of his success in law through intimidation in the courtroom.

After the workshop, Bob returned to work. While in a multimillion dollar negotiation, another attorney yelled at him, trying to intimidate him. A few days earlier, Bob would have fought fire with fire and yelled back! He would have intellectually and emotionally tried to dominate the other attorney. Instead, remembering that the 3R's were self-destructive, he replied to the angry attorney, "Thank you for having the courage to share your anger with me."

One of the most incredible things in his twenty years of negotiating occurred next. He instantly gained control of the entire room! Everyone knew that he was in control—of himself and the room. Bob won that day in a very big way!

Think how you can protect yourself and not resist at the same time. This brings us to the final "R," REVENGE.

REVENGE

Revenge is the attempt to get even or to settle the score.

The key word in this definition is "attempt." You cannot really get even because it is impossible to do so. You can fight back, and the person you are fighting can resent it, resist you, and seek revenge—which you feel you have to resist. It is an endless, destructive spiral. You cannot get even.

Let's look at how people attempt to get even at work. To get even, employees slow down, take longer lunch breaks than authorized, call in sick when they are not, "borrow" company property (theft), and participate in negative gossip. They do all this in an attempt to get even for resentments they carry towards the company.

How is revenge practiced in personal relationships? Common examples include: the silent treatment, denial of sex, running up the credit card, not doing chores, etc. Revenge is repeated a thousand different ways, all in an attempt to even the score.

The 3R's are self-destructive

Resentment, resistance, and revenge hurt *YOU*. What you put out, you get back. What you sow is what you reap. What goes around comes around. That's the law on the street as well as a Divine law.

Do you know children who get mad at their parents and try to get even by getting bad grades or getting messed up on drugs? That is classic 3R's! The child pays an incredible price to get even. Husbands and wives even use their children to get even with each other. This often leads to divorce, which hurts them as well as their children.

> **Resentment, resistance, and revenge hurt *YOU*.**

I have consulted with businesses where the 3R's are rampant, especially after a major downsize. Employee resistance can put a company out of business. It really is a dangerous and very damaging thought process. It is like the story of the Pied Piper who led the children of Hamelin to their deaths after the townspeople refused to pay him for ridding their town of rats.

If you operate according to the 3R's, you are headed for destruction! Think of a time when the sports world was rocked by strikes. The strikes were driven by the 3R's. Players resent owners for not paying them enough, owners resent player salaries that eat into profits, and in the end, nobody wins.

When the 3R's drive your decisions, reason and logic no longer matter. Children have religion shoved down their throats by parents and then cut themselves off from God in an effort to seek revenge. By doing so, the children lose any sense of spirituality. I consider this a huge price to pay!

How are the 3R's involved in your life?

Who or what are you resisting? What resentment do you carry with you on a daily basis? Where are you trying to get even? How much energy are you putting into self-destructive actions?

Silly, isn't it? "Tragic" is more the word I would use!

Is there ever any good reason to let the 3R's drive your actions?

Suppose I threw a cup of water at you. *Would that be a good reason?*

What if your boss fires you for no good reason? *Would that be a good reason?*

How about when a child is molested? *Would that be a good reason?*

What if a loved one is murdered? *Would that be a good reason?*

Whatever happens, no matter how cruel and damaging the circumstance, *using the 3R's is self-destructive*. It may or may not hurt the child molester, for example, but it

ALWAYS hurts the person who is ruled by the 3R's. I'm not saying you should never get upset, but if you allow being upset to lead to the 3R's, you will pay a higher price than you can imagine.

That price depends on your situation. The price might be

> **Is there ever any good reason to let the 3R's drive your actions?** *NO!*

physical or emotional illness, an unfulfilled relationship, divorce, living in the past and missing your present, rejecting God, etc. Whatever the price, it is too high a price to pay for self-destructive behavior.

How to avoid a life governed by the 3R's

Here are three solutions to living life free from the 3R's:

1. **Giving**

2. **Open, honest, and responsible communication**

3. **Fair fight**

The solutions are not comfortable if you are used to the 3R's and you want to get even for some slight. You might not feel like using these solutions because that means changing behavior patterns that feel familiar and comfortable. But why live your life governed by what you *feel* like doing when you could make choices based on what really matters to you?

Solution #1: Giving

Giving when in a state of resentment is an abnormal response, especially considering our programmed or subconscious thinking. When you give something positive to a person whom you feel resentment towards, does that mean the person is going to be nice in return? Not necessarily. Giving is not about manipulating the actions of others. It is not about trying to change other people. You don't control them.

So why are you giving? You are giving as a means of dealing with the 3R's. You don't want yourself, or anyone you care for, to pay that price.

Suppose someone in your office is inconsiderate to you. If you stay in resentment, you will not be as creative at the office. If you are in sales, you won't sell as well as you are capable of selling. Your company and your salary will pay the price. You'll go home and your family might pay the price because of your poor mood.

> **Learn to be a giving maniac!**

Instead, learn to be a giving maniac! Give when it is comfortable and when it is uncomfortable. Give when it looks like you will get back and give when it looks like you won't get back. Give when you know the recipient and give when you don't. Be a giving maniac not to be noble, but to be practical. All nobility is suspect. Give because there is a universal law that says what you put out, you will get back. As you sow, so shall you reap. *Give to get yourself out of the 3R's!*

The universal law, however, does not say it will come back from the same person, company, or source. Most people are so myopic that they look for the return immediately and expect it from the same person. When their giving does not immediately pay dividends, they believe the law is not true. This is a very nearsighted perspective.

Imagine being in a sleeping bag in a log cabin up in the mountains where it is snowing. The evening air around you is so cold that only your nose protrudes from the sleeping bag, and you can see your breath when you peer out. You then realize why it is so cold. There is no fire in the wood stove.

You look around and notice there is no firewood in the cabin. All the wood is outside where it is snowing. It is so cold in the cabin you can't will yourself to move your body out of the sleeping bag. You try to make a deal with the stove. "Warm me up and then I will gladly go outside and get some wood."

Does this sound ridiculous? Yes, but how often do we live our lives that way? In your relationship you say to the other person, "Spend more time with me (stove warm me up), and I will be more loving to you (I'll get you some wood)." Meanwhile, the other person is thinking, "Become more loving to me, and I will spend more time with you."

In the average company, management pays employees just enough to keep them from quitting. The employees work just hard enough to keep from being fired. In our rush to not be taken advantage of, each of us is waiting for the stove to first give us heat. It is the other way around. Give and then you will receive.

Solution #2: Open, honest, responsible communication

Let's suppose someone is a half hour late for an appointment with you, and you become upset. You decide to apply this second solution and communicate with the person. It might sound like this, "I feel upset. I feel like you don't respect me when you don't keep your agreements. I am angry."

In saying, "I am angry" or "I feel . . ." you are showing responsibility for your feelings by owning them. It would show irresponsibility to say, "You are making me angry!" That would be taking the viewpoint that something outside of yourself caused your feelings.[1]

Take responsibility and openly share your feelings without assigning the cause or blame to someone else. This can be difficult to do because we are used to blaming others for our feelings. Even if we accept responsibility for our feelings, and communicate openly and honestly, others may resist or resent us. When you communicate responsibly, you are not doing so to change the other person's behavior. That would be nice, but often times the other person will not change. *You are doing it to let go of your resentment so you don't have to pay a negative price for holding on to it.*

Today, people treat their resentments like frequent flyer miles. They don't say anything at the time of the resentment—they don't want to be rude or maybe are simply afraid. They quietly collect their "resentment miles."

Eventually, when the time is right, they cash in. There may be serious relationship consequences to this emotional outburst, but if they continue to hold in their resentment, they may become ill. Would it not be better to avoid the explosion and illness by releasing the pressure valve along the way? You do that by communicating your feelings in a responsible way.

Solution #3: Fair Fight

Most people, when they fight verbally, fight in a free-for-all manner. They say and do things to win the argument, not realizing they are destroying the relationship as a result. Fair fighting can actually help people build rela-

---

[1] The viewpoint of responsibility is discussed in greater depth in the next chapter.

tionships. It is great for parents and children, spouses, and even co-workers—people who know each other and who can agree to fight according to the rules.

Please note: The first two solutions can be used with anyone, but the "Fair Fight" solution can only be used with someone who will agree to the rules.

There are three Fair Fight rules:

Rule #1: You must agree on code words or signals. It might be "fight's on" or "red flag." When one of you calls it, you are both reminded that you are going to fight by the rules.

   It also states openly that a fight is going to take place! Have you ever been in a fight, but you didn't know you were in one? You knew something was wrong, but you couldn't put your finger on exactly what was going on. Using code words or signals places the fight out in the open.

Rule #2: There are two-minute rounds. Whoever calls the fight gets to talk first, but only for two minutes. The other person listens without saying anything or doing anything other than identifying with the experience of the first person. If you are the second person, you listen. Don't spend two minutes thinking of counter remarks or how to defend yourself.

   At the end of two minutes, the roles are reversed. The fight can go however many rounds you need to fully and openly communicate. Communication is a two-way process that involves sending and receiving.

   Some people are programmed to shut down when they get angry, while others are programmed to constantly spew their feelings. This rule forces both people to experience both modes at the appropriate time. One receives while the other person sends, and then vice versa.

In my experience, this puts the anger in perspective and reduces it, especially if the two parties remember to communicate their feelings responsibly. If they each own their feelings and do not blame the other person, then they are sharing their feelings.

Have you ever had an argument that starts over something small, like dirty dishes in the sink? Then it goes to something that happened last week. Then it goes to your mother-in-law. Soon, you are

> **Agree to the rules when things are going well.**

in a huge argument. When you fight fairly, you might still be angry after a couple of rounds, but you won't have the same intensity.

Rule #3: Both partners agree to not use any vulgarities. Vulgarities are degrading words meant to put down the other person. Vulgarities are poisoned darts aimed directly at the other person that are meant to sting and injure. Many times, vulgarities attack a person's physical appearance, race, religion, or ethnic origin.

Vulgarities drive most people directly to the 3R's as they increase resistance and resentment that lead to revenge. This is a surefire way to ruin a relationship. You may get caught up in the moment and say, "I hate you." That is you expressing a particularly strong feeling, but do not call the person you hate in that moment a vulgar name.

Agree to the rules when things are going well. Do not wait until you are in the heat of the moment to bring out this book and suggest using these rules, as you may find yourself eating the book. The rules may not even work the first few times you try them. Be patient any time you try a new behavior. It is no different than learning a new skill, like tennis. The first attempts will feel awkward, but once you get the hang of it, you will find it to be well worth the time spent on developing the skill.

These solutions may not feel comfortable or make logical sense initially, but I encourage you to use them and experience the results.

Begin to move away from the 3R's by thinking of three people for whom you feel the most resentment. Within one week, give something nice to one, communicate in an open, honest, and responsible manner with another, and set up fair fighting rules with the third. Do this whether you believe this will work or not. **There is no fairer way to gauge something than by results. Often harsh, but always fair!** By doing this, you will have an experience of whether this will work instead of an opinion.

Do not be concerned by their response to your actions, as this is not about them. You are not applying these solutions so that the person will like you or behave the way you want. This is not a manipulative maneuver to control them. *The solutions are for you.*

This is how you begin to release your 3R's and how you stop paying the price for living a life controlled by resentment, resistance, and revenge.

CHAPTER #4

Nobody can liberate
you, but you.

The Foundation of Liberty: RESPONSIBILITY

The tiny, desert-dwelling, sand wasp has a program or subconscious thinking that tells it to place its food outside the opening to its burrow before entering and then look around inside the burrow for anything dangerous. After finding nothing, the wasp brings the food inside its burrow and begins eating.

Let's add a scientist a few yards away, hiding behind a cactus. As soon as the sand wasp enters the burrow, the scientist races over and moves the food a few feet away from the entrance to the burrow, then hides behind the cactus. The sand wasp comes out of the burrow and sees the food has been moved. It pulls the food back over to the edge of the hole according to its instinct, then goes back down to check for danger.

The scientist again runs over and pulls the food away from the hole and returns to hide behind the cactus. The sand wasp comes up and sees the food has been moved and pulls the food back over to the edge of the hole and goes back down to check for danger.

Again the scientist runs over and pulls the food away from the edge of the hole. The sand wasp comes up and sees the food has been moved. It pulls the food back to the edge of the hole and goes back to check for danger.

How long would this continue? You could actually do this until the sand wasp died! It would continue pulling the food back to the edge of the hole and drop over dead of starvation. A startling fact! The sand wasp is a *victim* of its programs.

Our gift of choice

The genius of the human being is a God-given thing called *choice*. Sadly, most people are like the sand wasps. They give up their right to choose and defend their own programs or beliefs to their graves. They say things like:

- "That's just the way I am."

- "I've always been this way."

- "I can't communicate my feelings, it's just not me."

Ultimately, you must decide if you are a human being or a sand wasp. If you are looking for choices or options in life, it all begins with a concept espoused by Archimedes, the great Greek mathematician. He once said, "Give me a lever long enough, and I can move the world."

There is a lever that is long enough to move your world to an incredible place of excellence. Let's approach this concept from the backdoor and start with the victim viewpoint.

Viewpoint #1: VICTIM

Victim is the viewpoint where something has been done to you. The viewpoint that you have been exploited or taken advantage of and are not in control.

Think of a time when you played the role of a victim. Perhaps it was a car accident where the other person ran the red light. Maybe it was a business deal where you were misled or the other side reneged. Perhaps you put your all into a relationship, and the other person just left.

Pause here. Bring a specific time to mind and allow yourself to reexperience it. What did you feel: pain, anger, frustration, or hopelessness? How did you feel: embarrassed, foolish, humiliated, afraid, stupid, or overwhelmed?

Now imagine looking at a US nickel from the "heads" side. When asked to describe it, you would say that you saw the head of President Thomas Jefferson. Someone looking at the other side of the nickel would say that you were

VICTIM VIEW   RESPONSIBLE VIEW

clearly mistaken. They may even ask, "Don't you see a picture of the Monticello building?" Of course you don't.

Just as a coin has two sides, so we need to recognize that situations also have two sides. There are two viewpoints . . . yours is just one of them! Yours might not even be the right one. There might even be more than two viewpoints on a given issue, object, or circumstance.

This is just like the old story of five blind men who were asked to describe an object that they were not familiar with. They felt the object for a moment and one man said it was a long, thick rope. Another said it was a massive wall. The third said it was a pillar of stone. The fourth called it a tarp. Finally, the fifth blind man declared it was a large lizard. What was the object the blind men were describing? An elephant! Each man had been touching a different part of the elephant, and as a result, they had different viewpoints.

The victim viewpoint is one viewpoint. It is the "heads" side of the coin.

> **Just as a coin has two sides, so we need to recognize that situations also have two sides.**

Now, I'm going to ask you to take a deep breath and look at your story from a different point of view. Instead of taking the victim viewpoint, look at your own story from the responsible viewpoint. This is the "Monticello" side of the coin.

Viewpoint #2: RESPONSIBLE

Responsible is the viewpoint where you are "at cause" for your experience, out of the choice or choices you have made.

Reread that definition carefully. This is not fault or blame (a very different concept we will talk about later). For example, let's say Roma, my wife, and I have an argument. When I tell it as a victim, it would sound like this: "She didn't listen to me. She called me a name." It would be about what she did to me, which is the victim viewpoint.

When I tell it from the responsible viewpoint, I look at every choice I ever made that had anything to do with our situation. Maybe it was a choice that triggered the argument or caused it to occur. Maybe it was a choice made on another day that led us to the argument today. Looking for choices, I see several, including:

■ Who married my wife? Me! This doesn't make the argument my fault. However, if I had not chosen to marry Roma (one of the two best choices I have ever made, by the way), I would not have had an argument with her.

- Perhaps I chose, not consciously, to ignore previous signals or remarks she made indicating she was tired. Again, my choice does not put me at fault. It is a cause for the experience.

- Perhaps I chose to work or travel a lot and she felt ignored.

I probably could see one hundred choices I made that set up, or allowed, or outright caused the argument. Again, I am not at fault. The choices are simply "at cause" for my having the experience.

Pause again. Do your best to look for the choices you made that have to do with the victim experience you initially brought to mind. Put some effort into this, as it may not be easy. Take a few minutes to think or write down your thoughts.

What did you experience when you looked at your story from the responsible viewpoint? A variety of feelings might have come to mind. You could have felt surprised, resistant, excited, or numb, all at the same time! However you felt, you are in the mode of discovery, so learn from the experience.

Hopefully, you learned the most important lesson of all: *that the victim and responsible viewpoints have nothing to do with the truth!*

If you found yourself not wanting to look at the responsible viewpoint, *recognize that both viewpoints have nothing to do with the truth!* They have everything to do with what we experience, but NOTHING to do with the truth. For example, if I look at a white shirt while wearing my dark green sunglasses (victim viewpoint), the shirt will look green. If I look at the white shirt while wearing red sunglasses (responsible viewpoint), it will look red.

Does either viewpoint tell me what color the shirt is? No! But the different sunglasses have *everything* to do with what I see. The victim and responsible viewpoints have nothing to do with the truth, but everything to do with what we experience.

When you look at something from the victim viewpoint, you will likely feel negative (angry, foolish, frustrated, sad, etc.). You might feel there is no hope or no solution. Simply defined, *you cannot be the victim and find a solution.*

> **The victim and responsible viewpoints have nothing to do with the truth,** *but everything to do with what we experience.*

However, when looking at it from the responsible viewpoint, where you are "at cause" for your experience out of the choices you have made, solutions become possible. The possibility of a solution, perhaps to become who you would like to be, is a lot more exciting than that of no hope for a solution.

Is it guaranteed that the situation will turn out the way you want it to when you look at it from the responsible viewpoint? No! Perhaps you only have a 50/50 chance of making it work from the responsible viewpoint. A 50 percent chance is dramatically better than a 0 percent chance!

When you begin to look at events, situations, and circumstances of your life through the responsible set of sunglasses, you gain greater understanding, confidence, and self-esteem. Why? Because you are no longer the victim! And the odds of finding a solution go up dramatically.
Which odds do you want?

The average person looks at everything from the victim viewpoint. They are a victim of the economy, the weather, their schedule, their feelings, their bankbook balance, and all the other circumstances of life. On the other hand, leaders make decisions based on that which matters, rather than on the circumstances happening around them.

Even when your results are good, watch out that you don't ignore responsibility by saying the success was caused by something other than you. If the success was caused by something other than you, that is still a victim viewpoint and if circumstances change (new product, new compensation plan, new boss, etc.), you will not be able to recreate your success. Only from the responsible viewpoint do you have the power, ability, and option to recreate.

Choose responsibility

Choose to use the responsible viewpoint because A) it's more exciting and B) your odds of being able to create increase dramatically. Hold yourself responsible for the results in your life, not your parents and how they raised you, not the company you work for, not what someone else has said or done, not the economy, not the size of the town you live in, not the weather, and not the government. Hold yourself responsible for EVERYTHING—not because it's true, but because you want an experience that is exciting and full of possibilities.

Everything? Yes, everything. We at Klemmer and Associates have chosen to be responsible for creating "leaders who will create a world that works for everyone with no one left out." This is our mission, not because it is the truth but because of the excitement and possibilities we can see from the responsible viewpoint.

> **Hold yourself responsible for everything, not because it is true, but because of the exciting possiblities that the viewpoint creates.**

Responsibility is a choice. You cannot force someone to be responsible and you cannot delegate responsibility. You cannot delegate responsibility because it is a viewpoint. You can delegate authority because that is the right to make certain decisions. You can only encourage people to have the responsible viewpoint and let them choose.

Does responsibility mean you are at fault?

Being responsible does not mean you are at fault. This is a key distinction. Responsibility and fault are as different as houses and vegetables. If your map or subconscious thinking says that responsibility means fault, you will not look to see how you are responsible for anything.

Why? Simply because nobody wants to be at fault. Suppose my three children are young again and are running through the house. The six-year-old is in the way and the twelve-year-old bumps the fourteen-year-old, who falls into the table and knocks a glass of milk onto the floor. What is the first thing out of each child's mouth?

"It's not my fault, Dad. He was chasing me," says the fourteen-year-old. "It's not my fault, he was teasing me," says the twelve-year-old. Then, from the six-year-old, "It's not my fault, I was just standing here."

It may be okay for very small children to operate from this viewpoint, before they learn to take responsibility for their role in their experiences, but it is not okay for teenagers or adults to come from the viewpoint of fault or blame. Unfortunately, in our society, this is where most adults come from. If you doubt that, pick up your local newspaper. Choose any topic. Almost all the conversation will be about who is at fault. The realm of fault and blame offers no solutions. That is the price paid for wearing the victim set of sunglasses.

What is the responsible viewpoint with my children running through the house? The fourteen-year-old could say, "I chose to run through the room where the milk was." He did have other choices. He could have stopped running, watched TV, or played outside. From the responsible viewpoint, his choices set up or allowed an experience to happen. This *does not* mean the fourteen-year-old is at fault.

The twelve-year-old could have said, "I chose to chase him in the house." Again, there were countless other choices to choose from. This *does not* mean the twelve-year-old is at fault.

The six-year-old could also look at it from the responsible viewpoint. Maybe she chose not to say anything to her brothers because she was afraid of being picked on. This *does not* mean the six-year-old is at fault.

Even I, as the parent, made a thousand choices in this situation. I chose to have the children, I chose to raise my children in a fashion where it was okay to run in the house, and I chose to be somewhere else at the time. These choices do not mean that I am at fault. I gain power and possibilities and I feel better when I choose the responsible viewpoint. This *does not* mean that I was at fault.

Are you really at fault?

If your experience around any event includes anger, shame, or guilt, you are still thinking responsible means that you are at fault. *You can do that, but you will pay a price for it.* You will not move forward. Confusion comes when you think that being responsible means you are at fault. This creates anger, shame, and guilt, which will stunt your growth.

Make a list of all the things you have been victim to in the last year. Start with any goals you set that you have not reached. Make a list of at least ten experiences where you have been the victim. If you cannot come up with at least ten experiences, then add to the list that you are a victim of not being able to list your victim experiences!

> **Being responsible does NOT mean you are at fault.**

Perhaps you have been victim to your anger, to your lack of education, or to the amount of money you earn.

Now look at each event on your list from the responsible viewpoint. You will likely struggle to see how you are responsible for everything on your list, but does that mean you were not responsible. No. You still made choices, you just can't see those choices.

Remember, this is not about the truth or finding fault. It is about looking at both viewpoints of the situation. If you cannot see how you are responsible, then you have no power and will not see any solutions. Is that how you want to feel? Powerless? If not, look at your life from the responsible viewpoint.

I still struggle under certain circumstances to see how I am responsible for things, but I struggle in far fewer places now than when I started this personal growth journey more than twenty years ago. For example, the more I see how I am responsible for thousands of people starving to death every day, the more choices I can make to help end world hunger. You may be thinking, "I don't like the idea of being responsible for people starving to death." This reaction simply means you are still not "seeing" the responsible viewpoint. You are not at fault. You are responsible. When you see that, you can begin to see choices.

Seeing and being responsible

Think of the sunglasses again. If I have a green pair on and try to see white through them, what color do I see? Green. If I try to see the responsible viewpoint through a victim set of sunglasses, what am I going to see? Victim!

Have you ever heard someone say, "I don't want to be more responsible?" They say that because they are looking at the world, or their circumstances, through the eyes of a victim. From the victim viewpoint, responsibility feels like a heavy burden, duty, or obligation. To view the world and your circumstances through the responsible viewpoint is exciting, empowering, and liberating!

Years ago, we had a gentleman travel all the way from China for one of our seminars. For two days during the seminar, he did not say anything. When I asked him a question, he didn't reply. I realized that he could understand some English but he couldn't speak it very well or was too embarrassed to try. I then asked him when he would choose to see how he was responsible for what he understood and for what everybody else understood. He frowned. About fifteen minutes later, it was as though a light bulb went on for him. He removed his "sunglasses" and started to see things differently. He stood up and spoke Chinese. He had been victim to the fact that he didn't speak English.

He had started to see that he was responsible and began looking at his choices. He chose to take the class, he chose not to bring a translator, and he made the choices that set up and created the experience he was having. Now that he was looking from the responsible viewpoint, options opened up. One option was to speak Chinese!

Now I had a problem. I didn't understand him. I could look at it from the victim or the responsible viewpoint. I had made many choices to bring about this experience. I chose to hold the seminar in a location where people were more likely to come from Asia. I chose not to review the roster ahead of time. There were many other choices.

Soon, the man from China found a person at the seminar who could translate Chinese to English for us and English to Chinese for him. Interestingly, the translator had been in the room the entire time! If the man who spoke little English had not taken the responsible viewpoint, the translator would not have heard him speak Chinese. When we look through our victim sunglasses, we do not see options or solutions. Looking through the responsible viewpoint creates opportunities and solutions.

Choose to . . .

People often lump responsibility, accountability, and authority together, but they are different from each other.

- **Authority: the right to make certain decisions.**

- **Accountability: the willingness to pay the price for your choices.**

- **Responsibility: the viewpoint that you have choices.**

People often want authority, but they don't want to be accountable. Teenagers are great examples. They often want the authority to decide when to come home without a curfew, but are unable or do not want to be accountable.

Responsibility means you have choices. An extreme example of the consequences when people pretend they are not responsible and have no choices was in Germany during the reign of Hitler. He told people that he was responsible and they were not. Responsibility is not an either/or thing.

Everyone can take the viewpoint of responsibility all the time. The more we take the viewpoint that we are all responsible, the more exciting things are and the more we accomplish.

You cannot give up responsibility, because the choices you make create your experience. It is easy to pretend we don't have any choices when the price for holding the responsible viewpoint is high, but we always have choices. We may not want to deal with the consequences of our choices, but we have the choice.

When we work with teenagers, I often tell them they don't have to go to school. In the beginning, most of them argue. They say they have to. Anytime you feel you "have to," you are saying you have no choice and you are taking the victim viewpoint.

As we work with them, the teens begin to realize they can choose to not go to school. But what price would they pay? They would not have a formal education, but that's their choice. They might limit their career options, but again, that is their choice. They might go to a juvenile delinquent home if they don't go to school. They are choosing to go to school in order to not go to a juvenile delinquent home, which is their choice. *Understanding that you have choices, and understanding the consequences of those choices, is far more liberating than seeing yourself as the victim.*

You will have a completely different experience when you start to say, "I choose to" rather than, "I have to." In your life where you feel you "have to" do something, try saying, "I choose to" and keep saying it. You will have a completely different experience if you look at your choices from the viewpoint of responsibility. You will even begin to see other choices or options. As you examine them, you may decide that the price for making those choices is not as high as you once thought.

In fact, you might see the rewards you will reap when you begin to choose to do things differently. Because, in the end, it all boils down to the choices you make. Even if you let others make decisions for you, that too is your choice.

CHAPTER #5

Reality is for those
who lack imagination.

To Think Is to Create

There was a man who washed windows for a living. He wasn't very happy so he went to a positive thinking, pep-rally, motivational-type seminar. He got positive and motivated and went back to his job washing windows.

One day he was washing windows on the fifteenth floor, saying to himself, "I am a great window washer! I am a fantastic window washer! I am an incredible window washer!" While he was shouting these affirmations, his scaffolding broke. He started falling, much like the cartoon character Wiley Coyote. A couple on the third floor heard this positive thinking window washer as he passed, yelling to himself, "So far so good! So far so good!"

The moral of the story: *He still fell to the ground despite all his positive thinking.*

To think is to create

A simple way to state the philosophy we have been discussing is this: *to think is to create*. While it appears to be a simple statement, it is not an easy one to fully under-stand. You may have heard it explained many different ways:

- The Bible states in Proverbs 23:7, "As a man thinketh in his heart so is he."

- Napoleon Hill said, "Whatever the mind of man can conceive and believe, it can achieve."

- James Allen said, "A man is literally what he thinks."

To create a different life than you have, you must understand and internalize the truth behind the words: **to think is to create.** Ask yourself, "What does thinking really mean?"

Thinking positively did not create a new reality for the window washer. He still hit the ground. Obviously, there is nothing wrong with positive thinking. It's a good thing, but it just doesn't go far enough. Positive thinking won't fix a child on drugs, break a spending habit, or bail a company out of debt. Positive thinking just doesn't quite go far enough to create results in the way we mean results.

To better understand this fundamental premise of our weekend leadership seminar **Personal Mastery**, look at the three-level snowman here. This is a human being. You can use many different names to label the levels, so don't get hung up on the labels. Rather, begin to play detective and explore for yourself the ideas and concepts of each level.

The first level: This level has been called the head, the conscious mind, the lower self, and other names. This level consists of reason, logic, and your five physical senses: sight, hearing, smell, taste, and touch.

The second level: Have you ever used an alarm clock to wake up? If you were asleep, who heard the alarm clock? (Some of you may be saying that your spouse did, but if you were alone, who heard it?) Obviously, you heard it. There has to be at least two levels to you—one that goes to sleep and one that does not. The first level, or conscious mind, is the one that goes to sleep. The second level, or subconscious, is the one that never goes to sleep. It hears the alarm clock and wakes you up. This level consists of your emotions, memory bank, subconscious thinking, autonomic system (what runs your heart and lungs), subjective five senses, and intuition.

The third level: Unlike the first two levels, which are finite circles, the third level is drawn as a half circle to indicate the infinite. I choose to call this third or infinite level *God*, but you are free to call it another name. The "universe" or the "super conscious" are also common names for this level. One of the lessons I learned from my children is that the names they call me—Pops, Dad, Father, Step-Dad, or even Old Man—are not as important as the attitude with which they speak to me.

The positive window washer was thinking with his first level or his conscious mind, but conscious thinking rarely changes an outcome. Think hard and say out loud, "I am the president of the United Nations." Did this conscious (first level) thinking make you president? Simply thinking with your conscious mind does not create in reality the results you say you want. It takes something more powerful than simple reason and logic to achieve results.

To think is to create refers to your thinking at the second level. Your deep-seated assumptions exist at this level: who you are, how life works, what you think success is, and what it takes to be successful. This is where your sunglasses are kept and where the maps of your subconscious thinking can be found.

Challenging your beliefs

Do you think experience happens to you, or do you think you create it? Do you think you are a body, or something more than only a physical entity? It is not what is true, but it is what you think is true (your fundamental beliefs) that determines your idea of what your reality is for you.

> **It is not what is true, but it is what you think is true (your fundamental beliefs) that determines your idea of what your reality is for you.**

Consider travel. The decisions made about traveling were not based on the shape of the world—whether it was flat or round—but on what people thought the shape of the world was. When they thought the world was flat, they didn't go far, but when they thought it was round, they ventured much farther. Did the world change?

The following exercise illustrates how thinking creates our experience: **Take a piece of paper and write your full name on it as many times as you can, with your non-writing hand, in sixty seconds. Then and only then, continue reading this book.**

What did you experience? Some people did not do the exercise; some did it, but didn't go very fast; some were competitive; some worried about consistency; some just had fun; and some thought it was a stupid exercise. What did *YOU* feel? What caused you to feel that way?

I cannot tell you what caused you to feel that way, but I can give you several viewpoints or ways of looking at how you reacted.

When I do this exercise in a seminar, I keep telling people how many seconds are left and encourage them to go faster. I'll even count down the last few seconds. When I ask people what caused the various feelings they experienced, I always get a variety of answers:

- "Your tone of voice irritated me."

- "I was uncomfortable using my nonwriting hand."

- "I felt pressure because you were counting down the time."

- "I didn't experience pressure. I was simply curious to see what this exercise was about."

- "I had fun."

Because there are many different responses, you have to wonder: if we were all doing the same thing, why do we have so many different experiences or feelings? There are two fundamentally different ways that people think about the world and what creates our experience.

Belief #1: Doing = Experience

With Belief #1, what you or someone else is doing creates your experience.

Most people think this way. They say, "Of course I'm upset, my boss just yelled at me." Their viewpoint or set of sunglasses lets the actions of someone else create their experience. The boss yelling at them caused them to be upset.

Or so they say. "Of course I'm feeling insecure. I just lost my job." As if losing your job has anything to do with how you choose to feel! Most people think it does.

The problem with this belief is that if circumstances and people dictate your experience, you are at the mercy of everyone and everything! You have no power and never will have power.

Belief #2: Thinking = Experience

With Belief #2, your subconscious thinking creates your experience.

Remember the snowman? Your thinking in the second level or subconscious level (the one that never goes to sleep) is what determines your bank balance, whether you are single or married, happy or stressed out, and any other aspects in your life.

The advantage of Belief #2 is that it is usually easier to change your subconscious thinking than to change what other people, the economy, or your spouse are doing.

In the handwriting example, Belief #1 would say that pressure is caused by the person counting down, "25, 24, 23 . . . " (what they are doing). With Belief #2, the pressure is created by internal thinking since many other people heard the same counting down but did not feel pressure.

Belief #2 seems to be the more logical one. Also, it is easier to change our internal thinking than it is to stop someone else from counting down.

How do you change your thinking at the second level? It really isn't that difficult. People do it all the time, and so can you! The answer is *visualization*, the only "language" of the second level.

What is visualization?

To begin with, do you use visualization unconsciously (with no guidance by your first level) or do you consciously apply the use of visualization (with no guidance by your second level)?

Do you want your odds of success to be those of winning a lottery or do you want the odds stacked in your favor?

Obviously, you want to succeed, so consider this: if you don't apply visualization consciously, then your subconscious will apply it according to your beliefs, and you will recreate what you already have.

Clearly, visualization is a combination of both levels. It begins in the first level and then works through the second level. That is why it is so powerful.

Unfortunately, a lot of people hear the word "visualization" and immediately discount it. Some have a religious persuasion that categorizes visualization and imagination as "new age," while others discount visualization because they don't understand it. Whatever the reason, visualization is a neutral tool, much like money. Money can be applied for good things, such as building a home, or bad things, such as illegal drugs. Anyone can apply visualization techniques.

In 1996, I attended a Christian Leaders conference in Hawaii run by Harrison International Seminars. (It was fantastic and we now attend every year.) I was privileged to speak at the 1996 conference, and the speaker after me was Oral Roberts. He spoke for an hour and a half on visualization. Regardless of your opinions about him, would you classify this well-read Bible expert as a New Age guru? Yet he uses visualization.

> **Visualization is reproducing a picture in your mind of something you have seen.**

When I interviewed the pentathlon Olympic athlete and former world record holder, Marilyn King, she said, "No athlete in their right mind would attempt to compete at this elite level without using some form of visualization."

Even Thomas Edison used visualization as well as imagination to invent. Keep in mind that visualization is different from imagination. *Visualization is reproducing a picture in* *your mind of something <u>you have seen</u>.* Look at the floor, then close your eyes and see the floor. That is visualization, whether you see in detail or only have a blurry perception of the floor. The degree of detail is a skill level.

Now, imagine the carpet is made totally of thick, rich milk chocolate. Presuming you have never seen a chocolate carpet before, this is imagination. *Imagination is creating a picture of something <u>you have never seen</u>.* Again, you may see in detail or only see a brown blur. The degree of detail is a skill level. It doesn't matter. This is imagination because you have not actually seen a chocolate carpet.

How do you consciously apply visualization?

There are many methods and books on this subject, so I will keep it simple. Athletes see a picture of themselves throwing a perfect pass or sacking the quarterback. They often call it a "mental rehearsal." You can visualize an upcoming job interview or how you will complete a sale or even the perfect interaction between you and your child.

You can also engage in negative visualization, as most people do. For instance, you might have visualized an outcome, such as failing a job interview, that you do not desire and even had a strong emotional reaction. That's called fear! The hard part is visualizing what you don't believe is possible or real.

> **Imagination is creating a picture of something you have never seen.**

One of the simplest methods for visualizing in this case is called the "Screen of the Mind," and it's just like watching a movie. On your screen, visualize your situation as it is now.

For example, let's say you are renting an apartment and you want to own a home. You would see yourself in your apartment as it really is on a screen with a dark border.

Once you have your "as is" visualization set, change it. Visualize on your screen the image of whatever it is you want in a light frame. For your home example, you might see yourself living in a three-bedroom house, writing out the mortgage check with a big smile on your face.

That's all there is to the act of visualization.

As you use your "Screen of the Mind," visualize your current reality with a black border around it, much like the frame around a TV. I envision a large vanity mirror screen with lights around the frame. In my "as is" version, the lights are off.

Then, when you visualize what you want, change your screen's frame to a light color or, as I do with my vanity mirror screen, turn the lights on bright! The reason for this is that the subconscious always wants to see the image it believes is real **before** it accepts a new or replacement vision. See the old frame, and then change it. This helps your subconscious accept it.

Picture a big, street motorcycle. Imagine you want to go to the top of a hill, but your motorcycle has died at the bottom. Can you imagine pushing the heavy motorcycle to the top of the hill? A lot of work! Now, visualize that you are on top of another hill. Point the motorcycle downhill and watch the speedometer go! You are building momentum as you reach the bottom. Allow that momentum to carry you to the top of the hill.

It is much like that with your mind.

If you weigh 200 pounds and want to weigh 150, there will be a normal resistance for your mind to see yourself at 150 pounds. Let your subconscious go the way it wants for a short period of time, seeing you at 200 pounds on a screen with a dark frame. Then simply change the direction by putting a light frame around the screen and visualize yourself weighing 150 pounds.

> **We must learn to focus with our visualization on what we want and desire.**

As you are sowing these new pictures of what you want, your subconscious (your second level) will go to work creating the solutions. In the case of our weight analogy, you will find yourself becoming more disciplined, making different food choices, leaving food on your plate when you are full, getting more exercise, etc.

In the case of buying a house, you will find yourself discussing different options to finance a house, whereas before you weren't even open to the idea.

The role of your subconscious

You might be wondering:

■ "Do I have to work out all of the angles up front?"

■ "Do I have to know how to turn this new vision into reality?"

■ "Do I have to do everything right away?"

No, it is the job of your subconscious. Your subconscious is your problem-solving element . . . or is supposed to be! You put the subconscious to work by using pictures.

> **Visualization is the language to and from your subconscious mind.**

Sadly, most people try to solve all their problems or challenges at the first level, with reason and logic. The first level plays an important function, *but it is not there to solve problems.* Its job is to choose which pictures the subconscious should work on.

Have you ever been to a circus and seen someone riding an elephant? The person taps the elephant and it turns left. Another tap and the elephant moves a huge boulder.

Another tap and the elephant bends its head down to lift someone up.

What would happen if the human were to say, "I will do all the work today," and sent the elephant to its tent? The human would try to carry people around and move boulders. The human would be completely exhausted and mostly ineffective by the end of the day. This is exactly what happens with most people. They send their elephant (their number two part, their subconscious) to the tent and try to accomplish everything with just their number one part (their conscious mind). It cannot work because the subconscious second level is the problem solving part.

Reason, logic, and your five physical senses reside in the first level. This level can solve very little, yet it is where our education is most often focused. For example, if we want to buy a house, we usually try to solve the question of how to do it with our reason and logic. We look at income and financial outflow and decide, if income doesn't exceed expenditures, not to buy the house. *This is where average and mediocre thinking stops.* Successful people put the subconscious to work with visualization. The subconscious finds solutions outside of reason and logic.

Visualization is a way of circumventing the filters of your prejudices, beliefs, sunglasses, programs, and maps.

It is important to remember the specific role of the conscious and subconscious thinking and have them do their specific roles.

Without question, you cannot let the elephant run free! That would be chaos, but it happens when people send their conscious or first level mind out to lunch by taking drugs or consuming too much alcohol. In essence, their subconscious thinking is unrestrained.

The role of the conscious is to choose what the subconscious should work on solving!

Practice makes perfect

To be a master at anything, you need to practice. Great musicians and world-class athletes do not practice once in awhile or only when they feel like it. They practice every day, regularly, and consistently, and often at the same time and same place. They are disciplined . . . and you must be too if you aspire to walk in mastery and create a life of liberty.

Make a commitment right now to consciously practice visualization every day, ideally at the same time and location for at least the next thirty days. Visualize life as it is and life as you would like it to be. Conduct a mental rehearsal of the day going the way you want it to go as you achieve your goals. Practice visualization and be open to solutions from the subconscious. See what begins to happen in your life and judge this simple exercise on the results you create from visualization.

CHAPTER 6

He who knows why will always employ he who knows how.

Your Vision

One day while I was at work, my mentor (Tom) asked to see my life plan. I told him I did not have one. "Haven't you been listening to me?" he replied. He was referring to a book he had written called *Living Synergistically* where he instructs his readers to write out their life plan.

I explained that I had interpreted the concept of a life plan as a metaphor for having some sense of what one wanted to accomplish in life. (That sounded better than saying I was too lazy or undisciplined to write one.) Tom muttered a few choice words, something about expecting more out of me, and then said, "I'm sure you've at least written down some New Year's resolutions and therefore have a one-year plan!"

Embarrassed, I told him that I had set a few goals in my head, but had not written them down.

Tom ended our conversation by telling me to take some time off and write a life plan . . . and not to come back to work until it was completed. I had never before had a boss ask me to do this kind of assignment, but I was smart enough to know that if I did not do it and do it well, I might soon find myself on permanent vacation.

A couple of days later, I returned with several written pages and showed them to Tom. I will never forget the look on his face. He looked at what I had written and asked with a furrowed brow, "What is this?"

I told him it was my life plan.

"This is your life plan?" he asked with noticeable disappointment.

By now I was frustrated and confused. I had put a lot of work into my plan, but it was clear that something had gone wrong.

"This plan only covers the next fifty years," Tom said. (I was twenty-seven years old at the time and I thought a plan that covered me up until the age of seventy-seven included pretty much of everything that was important.) "Obviously, you don't understand anything I've told you about writing a life plan."

I took up the victim viewpoint to his criticism and went right into the realm of the 3R's (Resistance, Resentment, and Revenge), but I didn't stop there. My way of thinking about goal setting had been challenged, shaken to its core.

Who are you, really?

Do you think you are only a physical body with a limited life span? If so, that is probably why you are only setting goals for as long as you think your body will last. However, your body is not who you are! *You are a spiritual being in temporary possession of a physical body.*

If you understood that, you would be setting goals for not only the next five to fifty years, but also for the next one hundred years, five hundred years, and even for eternity! What you do today will affect your family, community, and world long after your physical body has turned to dust.

What kind of a game do you want to play with your life? Do you want to have a week-to-week game plan like most people or do you want a five hundred-year game plan? Listening to Tom, and finally hearing what he had been saying all along, completely changed the way I had been looking at goal setting within the concept of a life plan.

How large are your goals?

The depth and breadth of your goals play a huge part in what you set out to accomplish. If you do not dream big or set large goals, you will not be willing to pay the price to achieve your goals.

Remember the gentleman who traveled all the way from China to attend a seminar with me in Hawaii? His job was to introduce industrialization to a section of Communist China, and he wanted to industrialize it without polluting the area. He came to the seminar to find a way to meet that challenge. How is that for a large, long-term goal! Because his goal was large, he was committed to paying the price: the time and money spent for travel, the price of the seminar, and the price of navigating a strange land where he did not speak English.

> **If you do not dream big or set large goals, you will not be willing to pay the price to achieve your goals.**

In short, if you do not have a big dream and a large goal, you will not pay the price—the investment—necessary to achieve it.

All our clients in one of our divisions are network marketing companies and their representatives. I tell the representatives that one of the most important things they can do is to help new recruits discover big dreams and to set large goals. Otherwise, the moment new people meet rejection—and you know they will face it as they build their new businesses—they will quit. *People with big dreams are willing to pay the price it takes to face, endure, and overcome rejection.*

The "Why" behind the goals

You will not only want to set large goals and dream big, but you will also need to add one more important ingredient . . . a purpose or vision, which I call the *"Why."*

Goals are objectives to meet or achieve that can be measured, but a vision is never ending. It is the *"Why"* behind the goal that will affect your daily choice of activities.

Let's cut right to the chase and ask:

- Why are you living?

- What is the point?

- Are you living just to survive?

- If so, isn't that a losing battle?

- Are you living just for fun?

If you want fire and passion in your life, you need to discover a purpose. You need to find a vision and define the "*Why*" behind your goals.

We ask Fortune 500 clients who want to undergo major reorganization one main question, "Why?" In other words, what is the purpose behind their goal or dream? We know that all change will be greeted with a measure of resistance and turmoil. If the company undergoing restructuring does not have a strong purpose or "*Why*" behind its big dream, the executives and managers will become disheartened and eventually give up and go back to the old way of doing things.

The book of Proverbs states, "A people without a vision will perish." This is true for every individual, company, and nation. Anything without a vision or purpose will slowly die, whether it is emotionally, financially, or physically. Ask an insurance agent about the length of time the average man lives after he retires: *it's less than three years!* Many men set retirement as their goal but forget to visualize beyond retirement. When they reach retirement without having a new vision or purpose, they perish. They have no "*Why*" for living.

How many times have you heard of individuals who came from disadvantaged situations and rose to fame in professional sports? Though they were disadvantaged, they had big dreams to play professional basketball, baseball, hockey, football, or some other sport. But what often happens when they retire from the game? Many crash and burn. They might be flat broke and on the street and have a championship ring on their hand! They had a dream that they achieved, but they forgot to establish a greater purpose beyond their dream.

Three keys to working your goals

You have big goals, but where do you start? Use the keys that my mentor (Tom) taught me:

Key #1: Start with your biggest goal

Whatever your biggest goal is right now, at this very moment, start with that. Wally Amos, founder of Famous Amos Cookies, did not start out with a global dream. He started with a goal of one store, making it the best there was in the area. That seemed like a big goal at the time. Of course, once he established his first store and made it the best, he developed bigger goals.

You do the same, and remember not to compare your goal to the goals of others. It will only detract from your journey and deprive you of the joy you could experience along the way.

Key #2: Do not worry about your goal being the "right" one or not

For the moment, just proceed. You can change it at anytime. Imagine the captain of a ship in New York who refuses to set sail because he cannot make up his mind whether to go to England or Spain. On the other hand, if he decides to go to England and leaves the harbor, only to change his mind one thousand miles later and go to Spain, he is far better off than if he had never left New York!

I can remember one time saying to myself, "God, I know I'm good (Yes, I was arrogant!), but You have got to tell me what to do." I didn't think I heard a reply, so I did nothing for a couple weeks. Then one day I sensed something inside me saying, "Just get started, gain some momentum, and He will reveal the plan."

So that's what I did. I decided to get involved with a local politician because I wanted to make a difference in the community. I learned a number of skills in communications and networking. After a while, I realized that conducting **Personal Mastery** seminars was my real goal, the vehicle I could use to make a difference. But since I had worked for the politician rather than staying at home and doing nothing, I was further along in my goal than I would have been. My advice to you is . . . *get started now!*

Key #3: Find your "Why"

The only way to find your vision, your purpose, and your *"Why"* is to open up to God (or your version of God). I received more insight into this key, thanks to a student at one of my seminars, Jeff Chatsworth. Jeff, now a good friend, was using a New International Version (NIV) Bible and said his version used the word "revelation" instead of "vision."

Revelation is the process that reveals *that which already exists*, such as becoming aware of God's already established will. In other words, your purpose or *"Why"* is waiting for you to show up!

> The *"Why"* is the fuel that powers your goals and gives meaning to your accomplishments.

How do you find your *"Why"*? By quieting out the noises of the physical world we live in and praying or meditating until you discover your vision. Your vision or *"Why"* does not have to be a grand revelation. It need only be enough to get your feet moving today.

Making a life plan

In my experience, most people (75 percent) are merely activity oriented. For instance, parents focus on what they need to do: take the kids to the school, get the car in for a tune-up, shop for groceries, pick up the kids, help them with their homework, cook dinner, etc.

The same is true for a boss or an employee. The tendency is to be activity or task oriented.

Only a small percentage of people (perhaps 20 percent) are goal oriented. Ask a married couple what their marriage goal is and maybe one in five will have one. Most are simply doing the marriage.

Similarly, ask people what their income goal is for this year or for the next five years and most do not have one. They are simply doing their job.

If you were to ask people what their vision was, you would get a lot of strange looks. *Virtually no one (only 5 percent) has a vision or purpose!*

Setting goals

It is a well-documented fact that those who spend time identifying specific goals and writing them down are the ones who are most likely to attain their goals.

Therefore, the most powerful way to assist yourself with the goal-setting process is to write out your life plan. Start with your purpose, and then identify the goals you would like to accomplish over your lifetime and beyond. Then decide on the activities to accomplish those goals.

Take out several sheets of paper and write:

- **Goals you would like to accomplish in the next one to five years.**

- **Goals for the next five to ten years.**

- **Goals for the next ten to twenty years.**

- **Goals for the next twenty to fifty years.**

- **Goals for the next fifty, one hundred, and even five hundred years!**

Remember, whatever you do with your life affects the world and the people you leave behind for many years to come. You might laugh at this exercise and resist it like I did many years ago when I worked for Tom, but let me ask you, *"How big a game do you want to play?"*

Adding the "Why"

While it is good to set goals and have targets to aim for, you do not want to stop there. If you are only goal oriented, you will most likely burn out.

Do you know someone who is burned out? They set a goal to make $50,000 a year and they made it. Then they set a goal to make $100,000 a year and they made it. Then they set a goal to make $150,000 a year and they made that too. At some point along the way, they burn out.

Why? Because they did not determine, or they lost sight of, the motivating *"Why"* behind their goals. What was their purpose or vision? Why were they making the money in the first place?

When training our facilitators, one of the first things we ask them to do is to write down what we do, to list all the actions we take in our seminars. Then we ask them to figure out why we do them, such as why we have chairs set up the way we do, why we tell a particular story, why do we tell the story when we do, etc.

We recognize that when our facilitators know the "*Why*" and

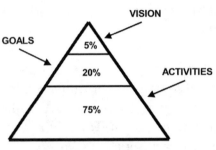

circumstances change, they can adjust what they are doing and still fulfill the original purpose. If they only know what to do, they will continue to do it even if it does not work or does not fulfill its purpose. *The same applies to everything you do!*

If you are part of the top 5 percent and have vision, does it not follow that you will have written down and set goals? Yes. And if you have vision and goals, does it not follow that you will engage in activities to achieve those goals? Yes.

One definition of *integrity* is the alignment of vision, goals, and activity. You are out of integrity when you are doing activities that are not in alignment with your goals or your vision.

Most people (the 75 percent) start at the bottom of this triangle with activities, which may or may not align with their goals.

This is precisely why a lot of people live unfulfilled lives. They take a lot of action, but it often does not fit their vision. This is why companies spend many thousands of dollars on mission statements—they are starting at the top and trying to work down.

Richard Brooke, CEO of Oxyfresh, wrote some of the best work I have ever read regarding vision in his book, *Mach II With Your Hair on Fire*. Do not let the strange title deceive you. It is an excellent book, written by a person who has achieved amazing results.

Choosing your activities

Take a moment to reflect on what you did yesterday. Visualize your day and briefly write down all that you did yesterday. This is important, so stop reading and do it now.

Next, examine each activity. Decide which ones were *productive* (produced income or moved you forward toward some goal or result) and which ones were simply **activity** (nonproductive, busy work, activities that took your time more than anything). Put a checkmark by each productive task, and then add up the total amount of time it took to do the productive activities and how much time it took to do the nonproductive activities.

> Goal-oriented people achieve their dreams. So set goals. Make them concrete. Write them down. Do it now!

I have had numerous entrepreneurs tell me they are working hard but are not making any money. When they explore how they are actually spending their time, they find that much of it is spent on busy work. They are "playing office" versus creating customers. Instead of picking up the phone and setting an appointment with a potential customer, they are making lists of things to do, organizing file cabinets, running computer diagnostics, creating business cards or brochures, etc. There is nothing wrong with being organized, but when it becomes busy work or a way to procrastinate, it costs you business. Procrastinators are often entrepreneurs without concrete goals or objectives.

A fulfilled life

What is the point of your life? Are you committed to busy work or productivity? Are your activities aligned with your goals and your vision? Have you established a life plan?

A life without vision or purpose can feel like a full life, but is it a fulfilled life?

The true mark of having lived well is to live on purpose and for a purpose. Taking the time to establish a clear life plan will empower you to live a life of joy and focus, to be a contributor to the good of your family life, your community, and the world at large, even long after you have departed from this physical world.

A worthy vision indeed!

CHAPTER #7

Balance is the key
to power and
peace of mind.

The Power of Balance

As you establish the goals and objectives that will support you in creating your vision, do so with a sense of balance.

Do you remember the Weeble Wobble toys of the '60s and '70s? No matter how hard you pushed them over, they would always pop right back up. They were curiously balanced, always able to right themselves.

You should possess the same ability, because balance is the key to power and peace of mind.

How square are you?

There is an old notion that you and I are like a square. (And to think you spent years trying to be hip or cool!) This notion suggests that we have four different natures or sides:

1. physical

2. emotional

3. mental

4. spiritual

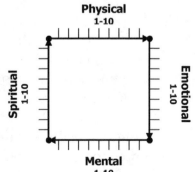

What makes a square a square, though, is the fact that all four sides are equal in length and at right angles to each other. When we develop all four sides of our natures equally, we achieve balance.

This balance leads to personal empowerment as well as inner contentment and peace of mind. Unfortunately, due to family dysfunctions, societal pressures, and many other influences, we often do not develop all four sides of our nature equally.

Take a few minutes to look at the four categories and do a quick self-evaluation. Give yourself an honest evaluation. Go ahead, no one is looking!

1. **Physical:** On a scale of 1 to 10, rate your physical development. A ten rating would represent you being the perfect weight, having great endurance, a normal blood pressure, etc. A one rating would represent the low end of the scale: terrible health, sick all the time, very high or low blood pressure, etc. *Rate yourself honestly.*

2. **Emotional:** On a scale of 1 to 10, rate your emotional development. How well do you express your emotions? A ten would represent perfect expression of your feelings, meaning that you can clearly express a wide range of feelings at anytime and that you express yourself in a way that is easily understood. A one on the

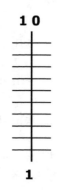

emotional scale would mean that you are terrible at communicating your feelings and have either totally suppressed your feelings or are wildly out of control when it comes to expressing your feelings. *Rate yourself honestly.*

3. **Mental:** On a scale of 1 to 10, rate your mental development. This rating requires some explanation. You may be tempted to use the degree of formal education you have attained to establish a high rating. I did when I first did this exercise, rating myself highly because I have a West Point education, made the Dean's List frequently, and have a Master's Degree.

My mentor asked me point blank, "If you are so smart, why aren't you rich? And why don't you have the romantic relationship that you've been looking for?" I realized that while I had a great deal of data in my head, it did not mean that I was mentally developed. I ended up giving myself a five because there were other things that needed evaluation to establish my intellectual state. Education is only a small part of the equation.

Give yourself a solid rating if you are highly educated and gainfully applying your education. If you are poorly educated and doing little or nothing to improve yourself, then your rating should be low. Include your income as part of your mental evaluation. If you are using your intelligence to earn $500,000 per year and you have a positive cash flow or you have accumulated wealth and are investing wisely, rate yourself high. If you cannot pay your monthly bills, give yourself a low rating.

Also, take into consideration the size of the problems you can solve. If you can solve global problems, definitely give yourself a ten! If you cannot sort out your attitude for the day, give yourself a low mark. *Rate yourself honestly.*

4. **Spiritual:** On a scale of 1 to 10, rate your spiritual development. Give yourself a ten if you have a terrific relationship with your Creator and if you know your purpose in life and are working to fulfill it. Rate yourself high if you always come from a "we" point of view, see your connection to the rest of humanity, and are able to make sure that others win as well. If you think life is all about you and what you can get out of it, your rating plummets. If you do not know your purpose or are not aware that you can have one, give yourself a lower rating. *Rate yourself honestly.*

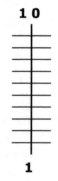

Putting it all together

Begin to put the four numerical evaluations together graphically to see what shape your square takes on by doing the following:

1. **Physical score:** Trace a horizontal line on the square box (on the next page) in proportion to the

number you gave yourself for your physical development. If you scored yourself high with an eight, then count over eight lines and put a dot at the end of your line. (Your line should be two spaces short of a perfect ten.)

2. **Emotional score:** Starting from the dot at the end of your physical line, draw a vertical line down that represents the rating you gave yourself for emotions. Count the exact number of spaces and put a dot at the end of your line.

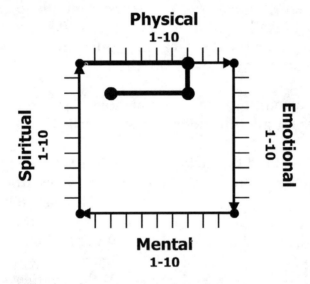

3. **Mental score:** Starting from the dot at the end of your emotional line, draw a horizontal line according to your mental development rating. Put a dot at the end of your line.

4. **Spiritual score:** Finally, starting from the dot at the end of your mental line, draw a line in proportion to your spiritual development rating to complete the square.

If you end up with something far from square, as I did when I first evaluated myself, then it is evident that your life is not balanced. If, by chance, your square is truly a square, keep in mind that there are a few more considerations before you give yourself too much credit for having a perfectly balanced life. A baby is also very balanced with a square that is 1 x 1 x 1 x 1, but no one would believe a baby "has arrived."

Life is about potential for growth in all areas. Is your square balanced at 7 x 7 x 7 x 7? If so, the question is, "How can you *remain* balanced and continue to grow in all areas?" And if you are already a 10 x 10 x 10 x 10, then you will probably discover that your potential scale for growth now moves to one hundred.

Life is a journey, not a destination. There are always avenues for growth and expansion.

When I first did this self-evaluation in 1975, the results of my "square" were less that impressive. *Physically*, I gave

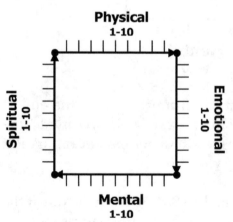

myself a seven because I was in the army, running three miles a day, and in good shape. On the *emotional* side, I gave myself a two. I grew up where strength meant suppression of your feelings. It was not okay to be angry. You never said, "I love you." Emotionally, I was a stoic. In fact, I may have been a bit too generous with a two rating.

Mentally, as I've already mentioned, I gave myself a five. *Spiritually*, I gave myself a zero because I had grown up with an "it's a dog-eat-dog world" attitude. If you do not look out for yourself, no one else will. The Vietnam War had recently ended, and I was cynical. If there was a God, then He was doing a terrible job. I did not have any purpose that I was conscious of, so I gave myself a zero.

As you can see, I was not at all in balance. It wasn't even a four-sided box!

What do you suppose most of my goals were at that time? More physical fitness and nutrition! More degrees in education! These are not negative goals, but they were driving me more out of balance. It was the law of diminishing returns; I was investing greater effort and experiencing little in return since I was already fit and educated.

After this exercise, I set emotional goals and spiritual goals. What happened? As I started to achieve my new goals, I became more content. I discovered an inner peace of mind. And, coincidentally, my income doubled! It was as if I had been stretching like a rubber band in only one direction. I needed to find balance *before* I could expand my life. Once I began to stretch the shorter areas of my life, I experienced growth and expansion in *all* areas.

Your square in regard to relationships

Using this model, let's suppose you are a man who grew up in a home where (for males), fitness, education, and money were all highly valued. Emotional and spiritual matters were not discussed and seen as not important. You were popular and in great shape and used this to get the pretty girls. You were going to be the breadwinner in life. Money talked; the rest walked.

Your square, if you grew up like this, would look like this:

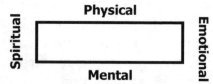

Now, let's consider a woman who grew up in a home where (for females) feelings were important, where intuition and a spiritual nature were valued, and where the importance of physical activity and education were downplayed. The messages she received were, "Don't bulk up or the boys won't like you. Don't be too smart or the boys will consider you a threat."

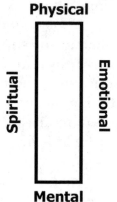

Take a look at the shape of the square of someone who grew up this way:

You might be thinking, "What's the big deal? Two people were raised differently. So what!"

Let's assume these meet, fall head over heals in love, and

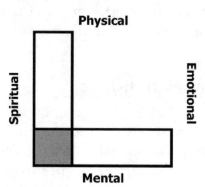

get married. Will they live happily ever after? I doubt it. Why? Take a look at how their squares overlap:

People only relate to each other in overlapping areas, and we do not have much overlap with this couple. He comes from reason and logic, while she comes from feelings. He often says to her, "You are not making any sense." She says to him, "Why can't you feel what I am talking about?"

If either one expands their square along the shorter sides, then the new square will encompass more of the other person. They will begin to relate more and have a better relationship—even if only one person grows along the lines of the other. If they both grow into each other's square, then the quality of the relationship will expand exponentially and will be enriched.

How to get results out of balance

Balance gives you power and peace of mind. To get results, you need to add one more ingredient: focus.

Focus is the key to gaining results. Visualize a 75-watt light bulb. The same amount of energy it takes to power that light bulb will also cut through six inches of steel! No extra power is required, but the energy needs to be focused in the form of a laser.

Combine balance and focus to produce maximum results!

Keeping each component of the square in mind (physical, emotional, mental, and spiritual) take the time right now to write down as many goals for yourself as you can. Do not be concerned about placing your goals on the appropriate side of the square. Just build your list of goals, as many as possible.

Then align each goal with the side of the square that, from your viewpoint, best relates to each goal.

Now look at your goals in relation to the length of the sides of your squares. Do you see where your current priorities are? Do you see where your priorities should be? What can you do to stretch yourself in the direction or directions in which you need to be stretched?

Where can you begin to *focus* your energy in order to achieve greater *balance*? Focus and balance equal harmony and produce maximum results!

CHAPTER #8

Every man is an island
... but no man is an
island unto himself.

Oneness versus Separateness

Many years ago, I conducted a workshop for religious leaders. More than fifty individuals came of various theologies, including Catholics, Jews, Mormons, Pentecostals, Methodists, Unitarians, and Seventh Day Adventists.

It was their impression at the beginning of the workshop that I was going to discuss theology with them. Instead, I planned to talk about the day-to-day things that mattered to them: preaching God's Word more effectively, having a happier home life, reducing stress levels, and enlarging their congregation.

To do so, we also had to explore the beliefs that prevented us from achieving what mattered most. It proved to be a very interesting time!

Though all of them professed great love, some of them would not sit next to each other when the workshop started. They all talked about mankind as one family, yet many of them began the seminar as if they were at war with each other. During an exercise on leadership, one group laughed at another group for not listening. They were not doing what they knew to do, much less practicing what they preached.

We talked about the difference between what we think we believe and what we actually believe. (This can be a harsh awakening!) It is all part of exploring our beliefs—the lenses in our sunglasses—and then looking for ways to better our situation. Ideally, the end result will be a win-win situation.

During the conference, a Seventh Day Adventist minister and a Jewish rabbi mentioned how their children were not able to participate in the community soccer league because the games were held on Saturdays, the holy day of worship for both their faiths. Right there, the minister and the rabbi decided to form a joint Jewish-Seventh Day Adventist soccer league that played on Sundays. The church leaders and the children who attended their churches all experienced a win-win.

What exactly is a *Win-Win*?

Win-Win has become a popular buzzword for an old idea, but it simply means finding a solution that allows all parties involved to receive an equal and satisfying benefit.

Steven Covey popularized the phrase in his book, *Seven Habits of Highly Effective People*. Buckminister Fuller did groundbreaking work on this topic as well. Martin Luther King talked about his vision of all races having food, shelter, and living in harmony. Mahatma Gandhi worked on peace for the British, Indian, Hindu, and Seiks. These world leaders believed in *Win-Win* thinking.

So why aren't more people *Win-Win* oriented? I believe it is due to a fundamental perception of reality that most people hold. They believe that we are separate—separate genders, races, ethnicities, religions, philosophies, educational approaches, political movements, and so on.

Once this set of sunglasses or subconscious thinking of **SEPARATENESS** is in place, it filters everything through an *us versus them* mentality: Christian versus Muslim, Conservative versus Liberal, rich versus poor, talkative versus shy, old versus young, American versus non-American, and on and on.

Once this way of thinking has taken hold, no matter how many teamwork books you read, you will not approach life from a Win-Win viewpoint.

As you know, behavior is determined by our programming or subconscious thinking and not by what we want or by what we know is good for us. Incidentally, it is definitely not shaped by what we are told to do.

> **Do you see *one* or do you see *separate*?**

In a world of separateness, it is labor versus management, my department versus your department, individuals versus individuals, state versus state, countries versus countries, all fighting for the same things.

What do you see?

If you have been to the beautiful island of Maui, you might

have heard about the small island nearby called Kaho'olawe. Kaho'olawe is not only uninhabited, it has been used as a bombing range by the military for many years.

If we were sailing down the channel that runs between them, we would see two different islands. One is tall; the other is short. One is lush; the other relatively barren. One is populated; the other is not. One is alive; the other is dead. There would be a long list of differences.

Imagine there is a giant plug at the bottom of the ocean—like the plug on a bathtub—and suppose we pulled the plug. All the water would drain out, leaving us with . . . *one island!* (On that note, the entire Earth is one connected land-mass.)

This is what we call the *REALITY OF ONENESS* versus the *ILLUSION OF SEPARATENESS*. The reality is that we, like the land, islands, and mountains, are all connected, even though we cannot always see what connects us. I am not saying we are not separate individuals. We are separate, unique individuals who also happen to be connected.

Are we all connected?

Do you think you are connected in some unseen way to your boss, almost like an umbilical cord? I suggest that you are. In addition, I suggest that you are connected to everyone you know, whether they are friends or enemies.

If you are indeed connected to everyone, does it make sense to compare yourself negatively to others and to put yourself down? No, it does not. Nor can you put someone else down because that is putting yourself down!

The concept of connectedness is like seeing the world through the old adage, "Givers Gain, Takers Lose." What you give out you get back. What you sow you also reap. What goes around comes around.

If I pretend I am an island separate from others, then I can live in a world of indifference and do whatever I please. I can commit acts of violence or live smugly as I accumulate wealth at your expense. *However, once I discover that we are all connected, I must act according to my new sense of reality.*

What are all the ways you pretend you are separate? Be honest. Do you only feel connected to those who agree with you, dress like you, have the same skin color as you do, or live in the same town or neighborhood? Perhaps you only feel connected to those who share your values, religious beliefs, or economic status.

How would it change your viewpoint if you saw separateness as fake and unreal? How would you change if you believed you were totally connected? Would that make you more or less responsible for your actions and for others in general?

Because of separateness, companies and governments act as if they are separate from the earth. How unrealistic is that! That is why entire nations have been deforested, rivers polluted to the point that nothing can live in them, and soil so overused that famine

> **Win-Win is an option. It has the greatest potential but carries the greatest risk.**

is common, and this doesn't even count the numerous examples of ethnic cleansing.

In contrast, the Native American Indian culture, for example, sees a connectedness between the earth and all mankind. This is reflected in their language, calling the bear and the fox their "brothers." If we too had a global consciousness, we would have much greater respect for each other and for the world in which we live.

What is a *Lose-Lose*?

Do your actions today benefit everyone or do they only benefit one sector of humanity at the expense of everyone else? Because our mission at Klemmer and Associates is to create "leaders who will create a world that works for everyone, a world where no one is left out," this requires giving and finding **Win-Win** solutions. It also leads to maximum gain for everyone!

An isolationist policy or separateness philosophy, on the other hand, is an "us versus them" approach. It may appear to be a **Win-Lose** scenario initially, but it actually leads to a **Lose-Lose** outcome.

Let's examine this philosophy in a business situation. I am sure you have seen four gas stations on each corner of an intersection. (We could use four airlines, four fast food restaurants, or four retail stores in this example.) Have you ever seen what happens when gas station A cuts its price by a penny a gallon? Gas stations B and C also cut their prices by a penny.

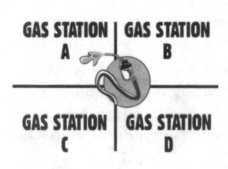

Then gas station D cuts its price by two cents. Gas station A then cuts its price by 4 cents.

Most people think this is "competition." I suggest it is not. It is suicide. Why? Because a couple of the gas stations will eventually go out of business if they keep it up. The two stations left in business will then raise their prices once again in an attempt to recover some of what they lost in the price war. It is a *Lose-Lose* game. The customer initially gets a better price, but the customers lose when service is reduced. Safety might even become an issue as the gas station owners cut corners to compete.

Now, suppose gas station D tried a different strategy and did not cut their prices. They focus on giving—increasing their service and adding value. You drive into gas station D and immediately an attendant greets you with a smile, pumps your gas, checks the air pressure in your tires, and cleans the windshield. No self-serve here, all this and you were just looking for directions!

Additionally, someone else inspects your vehicle, rolls under your car on a dolly to see if anything needs fixing. If he finds a few items that need repairing, he says, "The items marked in blue are the ones we'd appreciate you letting us take care of. We have great prices and excellent service. For the ones marked in red, we recommend you go to several other companies listed on the back."

Would you go to this gas station again? Of course you would. Why? Because they are doing whatever it takes for you to win, even if it means sending you somewhere else.

Win-Win is a maximum-gain solution

Wouldn't you agree that the approach of gas station D would be a rather abnormal way of running a business?

Would you tell your friends about gas station D? Of course you would, because you want your friends to win too.

Now remember, the price you are paying for gas is higher than the other gas stations that cut their prices. But soon you, your friends, your family, and their friends and family are all going to gas station D. How is gas station D doing financially? Great! They win and their customers win, but it does not stop there.

The owner of gas station C can see the owner of gas station D is doing well financially while everyone else is losing money or struggling. Suppose owner C asks owner D what the secret is. If owner D comes from a separateness mentality, owner C will be sent packing.

This is what I call "middle management syndrome," but it happens at all levels of management. It is a way of thinking that believes, "I won't tell you what I know because if I do, I will be out of a job" (or prospects, or investment opportunities, etc.). This is separateness thinking.

> **The game you want to be competitive in is the game of service.**

Owner D, however, believes in giving to others and lives life from that perspective. As a result, owner D explains to owner C, "You need to give more. Offer more service." Perhaps they discuss this over lunch, with owner D picking up the tab. Why not? Owner D can afford it and it is yet another way to give.

When owner C puts the secret to work and business begins to grow, does gas station D lose customers? No, they actually gain customers. Why? Because the game of service is infinite, while the game of price is finite. You can only cut prices so far before you are losing money. *Service, however, is infinite.*

Some of the services that gas station C provides would be the same as those gas station D provides, such as smiling attendants and pumping the customer's gas. But since service is infinite, some of the services would be different. Perhaps gas station C would repair transmissions and gas station D would repair brakes. Together they would increase the total number of customers that come to that corner and they could refer customers to each other.

Some of our corporate clients with large sales forces have benefited enormously from using this principle. Many had previously tried to cut costs by reducing commissions, but in the end, they ended up working harder and making less money. Once they learned to maintain their prices and become giving maniacs, they earned more money.

Ultimately, what you want to give is extraordinary service. This practice of giving requires you to know what is important to your customers (employees, friends, family, etc.). It is not just giving randomly, giving only what you want to give, or giving a few items traditionally given away in your industry.

For example, can you imagine a bunch of managers sitting around brainstorming how employees could make more money instead of brainstorming how they can squeeze a few more hours of work for less pay out of their employees! That would be of incredible service. Can you imagine employees looking for ways to make life easier for their manager or boss, ways that allow the boss to work fewer hours, spend less time putting out fires, and more time accomplishing goals that lead to *Win-Win* situations for all!

In the average company, however, nobody looks for **Win-Win** situations. The subconscious thinking is based on separateness, which usually leads to **Lose-Lose** situations for owners, managers, employees, and customers.

Is there enough pie to go around?

Think back to your childhood for a moment. If you happened to have pie for dessert and also had brothers or sisters, what went through your head as the pie was being cut? I bet I can tell you. You wanted the biggest piece of pie or at least you wanted your fair share. With every piece of pie cut and passed around the table, the less pie remained.

This is what is known as a "fixed pie" game. There is only so much to go around. If you do not get yours, you will get none. When we see the world through these parameters, we treat <u>**everyone**</u> and <u>**everything**</u> as if there is not enough to go around.

Some things might be fixed, such as dessert and price, but other things, such as love and service, are infinite. Regardless, if we believe there is not enough to go around, then we will be unwilling to love to the fullest, give to the fullest, or live to the fullest. It is a limiting thinking that affects us in every way.

How to bring about change

The only way this "fixed pie" subconscious way of thinking (or any other deep-seated paradigm) can be changed is through emotional involvement and repetition. Intellectually knowing about connectedness is not enough. You can know about something and not know it. You can know about a romantic kiss and still have never experienced one.

This is why we conduct workshops, such as **Personal Mastery**, **Advanced Leadership**, and **Heart of the Samurai**. During these workshops, individuals begin to see the world, themselves, and concepts such as commitment, loyalty, responsibility, and giving in new ways. It is an amazing experience. The experience helps individuals reevaluate and shift their fundamental subconscious thinking (sunglasses) about reality.

Rarely does anyone's fundamental thinking change simply from reading books or listening to tapes. The books and tapes provide repetition, but not emotional involvement. The best vehicle of change is a combination of the two.

The more emotionally involved you become, the less repetition is needed to create lasting change in your subconscious thinking. Translated, this means that the fastest change is possible when you are emotionally involved.

They say it takes twenty-one days to break a habit, but in my experience, this is not true. I have changed some habits as fast as I can snap my fingers, while I have spent years trying to change other habits. When it comes to making substantial changes (the breaking of a serious habit, for instance), the level of emotional commitment involved is key.

> The more emotionally involved you become, the less repetition is needed to create lasting change in your subconscious thinking.

Do you know someone who does not exercise but wants to? It can be incredibly difficult to move from a lack of activity to a state of regular exercise. It requires a great deal of emotional commitment to develop a new habit like working out regularly. Health clubs know this because they have a difficult time keeping clients. They try all types of financial gimmicks to keep members involved because they know it takes longer than twenty-one days to develop the workout habit. They try to get new members to commit (pay membership fees) for at least three months. Even then, turnover is high. Even members who sign up for a full year often quit after a month. They simply cannot break their habit of inactivity.

Now consider someone who has had a heart attack. That is usually an emotional bombshell. It does not take many heart attacks (seldom more than one!) before bad habits are replaced. However, in some cases, I have seen people who had heart attacks or strokes who continue to shove fatty foods in their mouths or continue to smoke cigarettes or who refuse to engage in the moderate exercise that recovery requires. Perhaps you know people like this too. This is a major clue as to how deeply ingrained and destructive subconscious thinking can become!

Unless you are very committed, your programming or subconscious thinking will beat you every time. *It is you versus your beliefs!* How many times have you tried to break a habit or start a new habit? Repetition and emotional involvement are required to break the old pattern.

Why not start today?

Having a sense of purpose or vision to reach certain goals will be a great help in bringing about the change that you want. It will also help if you see yourself connected to everyone else, rather than living your life with a separateness mentality.

You have been endowed with tremendous potential! So, up your commitment to change your life. Change your thinking, change your actions, change your sunglasses, and change your point of view. Start today!

CHAPTER #9

> "Every day man crucifies himself between two thieves—the regret of yesterday and the fear of tomorrow."
> – *Benjamin Disraeli*

www.klemmer.com

An Action Attitude . . .
First Day, Last Day

QUESTION: Do you regret more what you have done or what you haven't done?

Once upon a time, there was a man who was in pursuit of his dream. The man's dream resided on top of a great mountain, so the man began the climb with vigor, even sprinting up the mountain in his excitement. But you know how mountains go. They get steeper and steeper. Soon the man was not sprinting; he was walking. Soon he stopped walking and began to crawl. The man was obviously very committed, but finally he could not go another step, and he collapsed on the side of the mountain.

Along came a little traveler, humming and singing (I imagine the little traveler as wearing lederhosen and hiking boots). He asked the man what he was doing and the man replied he was climbing to the top of the mountain. The little traveler replied, "No you are not, you are resting."

"Well, of course I am resting," said the man. "Climbing to the top of the mountain is hard work."

The little traveler then asked, "If you want to go to the top of the mountain, why are you carrying that fifty-pound sack of manure on your back?"

The man was shocked. "There is no sack of manure on my back," he replied. But, sure enough, when he felt his back, he discovered a heavy sack. "Well, I never knew that was there!" he said with surprise.

The little traveler asked him if he wanted to keep it. "Of course not," the man answered.

"Well then, throw it off the mountain," said the traveler.

The man did. Instantly, he felt revitalized and refreshed! With renewed energy, the man began once again to sprint up the side of the mountain, leaving the little traveler in a cloud of dust.

But you know how mountains are. Just like life, they tend to get steeper and tougher to climb, and soon our man was huffing and puffing as he went. He was very committed, but he once again collapsed in exhaustion. Along came the little traveler, humming and singing the same tune.

"What are you doing?" he asked the man.

Our man replied that he was still trying to climb to the top of the mountain, but he had to take a moment's rest.

The little traveler asked him why in the world he was balancing a fifty-pound pumpkin on his head while he was trying to climb the mountain. The man said, "That's ridiculous. There is no pumpkin on my head!" But when he checked, to his embarrassment, he found a fifty-pound pumpkin on his head. The man started to examine it. He wondered how long it had been there. Had it been there his whole life?

The little traveler asked, "Do you want to keep it?"

"Of course not!" the man replied, and he threw the huge pumpkin off of the mountain. He then was able to move forward with ease and soon reached the top of the mountain. Without his burdens, he was able to reach his dream.

The moral of the story is this: *How many sacks of regret and pumpkins of fear are you carrying as you climb your mountains and attempt to reach your dreams?*

Knowledge is not enough

Have you heard, "Knowledge is power"? The truth is, APPLIED KNOWLEDGE IS POWER. Our logo is K + A, which stands for Klemmer & Associates, but it also stands for *Knowledge into Action*.

So many times the twin thieves of fear and regret poison and paralyze us. We have an antidote! It is a belief that states: *"Today is the first day and the last day of the rest of my life."*

This idea is a vaccine for the disease of inaction caused by regrets and fear. When we apply it, we release regret and fear and become excited and energized. We move forward, up the mountain, and toward our dreams.

PART ONE: Today is the first day of the rest of your life.

If today were the first day of our lives, we would not have any regrets, would we? No, because we would not have had time to accumulate regrets.

Your first day at work

Do you remember your first day at work? That day was most likely filled with a great deal of anticipation and excitement. Your attitude was extremely positive. "Hey, lay it on me. Let me prove to you how much I can do!"

A first-day attitude is exhilarating and exciting!

What happened after you had worked at your job for a few months or years? Perhaps you lost the passion you once had. Perhaps you felt as though your boss played office politics by rewarding others for work you did, or maybe your boss did not pay you what you were worth. Perhaps you lost your enthusiasm and stopped showing up early. Maybe you began to even show up for work late or take unwarranted sick days.

The following idea might seem silly, but here is what I want you to do. Go to work tomorrow as if it was your first day again. Choose to look at your job through your first-day sunglasses, the same ones you wore your first day on the job. See what happens!

Your first date

Can you remember the attitude with which you approached your first date? Can you remember the heightened anticipation? You were nervous, maybe, but you were also excited. That is a first-day attitude. But what happened after you had been in relationship with that person for years? Perhaps you both accumulated regrets that you still carry. One of you forgot an anniversary. Someone said or did something hurtful or unwise. You let an opportunity to express your feelings pass by. Soon you were carrying a few pounds of manure on your back and the relationship did not seem so exciting anymore.

If you are in a romantic relationship, then pretend you are meeting your significant other for the first time today. If that means you would dress up or buy them flowers, then do that! Forget whether you think the other person deserves it. That thinking is based on the past. Simply choose to look at the relationship through a set of sunglasses called "today is your first day." In my experience, most marriages that end in divorce do not end in one big, sudden blow out. They die from the slow leaks of resentment and regret.

Your new baby

Do you have children? Do you remember the first time one of your children rolled over? Of course you do! "Honey, she rolled over! Did you see that form? She's going to be an Olympic gymnast." What happened after your child rolled over one thousand times? You were not as excited anymore. And after they messed up your new carpet? And after they started back talking or goofing off in school? Maybe you lost that first-day attitude

> **The first-day attitude is an exciting attitude with no baggage to hold you down.**

and started saying things like, "Would you just let me read the paper?" Today, even if your children are grown, pretend it is your first day with them. Pretend you are seeing them for the first time again, and see what happens.

What a relief a first-day attitude is. No grudges. No regrets of a childhood that was not the way we wanted. No regrets over relationships we let slip away or over ones that did not work out. No regrets about poor decisions, inappropriate choices, or foolish actions. This first-day outlook is refreshing and exciting!

Have you ever seen children watch a movie over and over and over? They are so excited each time! This is what a first-day attitude looks and feels like.

PART TWO: Today is the last day of the rest of your life.

Next, consider today to be the last day of the rest of your life. This is a call to action! It is an attitude of urgency. Not panic, but definitely a "do it now" attitude.

If you had only twenty-four hours to live, you would not put off important things until tomorrow because there would be no tomorrow. If you knew your spouse had only twenty-four hours to live and you saw he or she was upset, would you get upset as well? Or would you say, "Hey! We don't have time for this. Let's do something that matters. Let's talk about what's important to us. Better still, let's do what is important to us."

Are you doing what you deem important every day of your life? Are you living as if today were the last day of your life? Isn't that how you would prefer to live your life? If so, do it. Do it **now**! Instead of watching TV, instead of waiting for the "right time" to do what is important to you, instead of waiting until you feel more comfortable or the time is more convenient, **DO IT NOW**!

Put down this book now and communicate something important to someone you love or care about. Do it now. Take on a last-day attitude. If you only had twenty-four hours to live and your children wanted to do something with you, would you put it off or would you do it now? Would you not approach your children and your life with the urgency of a last-day attitude?

When do people "get it"?

Do you know when most people develop a last-day attitude? When they perceive it to be their last day. Someone gets seriously ill and starts acting with urgency—about their health, their financial planning, and their family. Sadly, people seldom develop a last-day attitude until a doctor says, "You only have days or weeks to live."

Instead, we are governed by an attitude that says, "There is plenty of time to live, plenty of time to do the important things." If you have young children, it is so easy to believe that you will have plenty of time with them. Your attitude might be: "I'll work hard now and catch up with them later."

But how much time will you really have with them? You cannot know for sure. Live life as if it is your last day. Live with a sense of urgency (last day) and excitement (first day).

Guarantees, guarantees, guarantees!

Why do so many of us suffer from the attitude of inaction? I believe it occurs because we live in a country where so much seems guaranteed. Most of you would not buy a car, stereo, or appliance without a guarantee of some kind. Sometimes in my seminars, I have people pull out their wallets and purses and count the guarantees they carry with them. They are astounded. Credit cards guarantee we can buy things. ATM cards guarantee we can retrieve money from our account at any time. Pictures guarantee memories. Life insurance guarantees that our heirs will be provided for. Medical insurance guarantees we will be medically cared for when sick. Library cards and drivers licenses are even a type of guarantee.

Guarantees give us greater liberty, but with so many guarantees, we begin to assume that we are guaranteed to live until a ripe old age. Add in the so-called medical breakthroughs we hear about all the time, and we begin to assume a healthy life is guaranteed almost indefinitely.

Have you ever been in an argument, and said to yourself, "I do not want to handle this now, I'll handle it later?" What if, instead, you took the viewpoint that today was the last day of your life? Might you deal with it immediately?

Would you even go to work today? If not, then maybe you are in the wrong job! If the only reason you go to work is to collect a paycheck, you are blowing it. You are trading your life away for a very small price. On the other hand, if your work is a vehicle for your self-expression, you would spend a part of your last day at work. If your life was about making a difference and your work allowed you to make a difference, then you would spend part of your last day at work because it provided you with an opportunity to achieve your goal, to fulfill your vision, and to climb to the top of your mountain.

Lack of vision

Perhaps there is another reason we do not live as if today is the last day of our lives. We have not formulated a vision. We are engaged in busy work, not productive life work.

There are plenty of jobs out there or businesses you can run that will let you make all the money you want. But what is it you want to do? Do you want to find a vehicle to fulfill your purpose? Do you have a purpose? Your life is too valuable to trade for anything mediocre. *You are too valuable for that!*

When people do not reach for their dreams every day, then each day a piece of them dies. For most, it is a slow process, so they are unaware of the price they are paying. Then one day, they realize they are walking zombies. They are survivors—existing in life, but not living a full life. Benjamin Disraeli wisely wrote, "Every day man crucifies himself between two thieves, the regret of yesterday and the fear of tomorrow."

Take action today

If today were the last day of your life and you could have or do any ten things you wrote down, what would you want and what would you do?

Take a minute to write down your answers. If you wanted to travel around the world, even though that would take longer than twenty-four hours to do so, write it down. If you wanted to discover the cure for AIDS, write it down. If you wanted to earn a million dollars, write it down. Anything you want, you can have. Anything you want to do, you can do.

Write down your top ten and write them down before you read any further. Take this seriously.

1.

2.

3.

4.

5.

6.

7.

8.

9.

10.

Did you write down ten things that you want to do? If not, you do not have a last-day attitude. Stop and do it for your own sake. This is part of developing a last-day attitude, a sense of urgency about what is important in your life. If you made your list, congratulations! You are already developing a last-day attitude.

And now, the next step is to take action on one item. *Right now!* If you wrote something grandiose, like solving world hunger, then look through the telephone book and find an organization that feeds the hungry. Call and volunteer some of your time. You will not solve the problem now, but you will be taking that first step up the mountain.

If you do not take that first step, you will never reach the peak where your dreams reside. So, take action NOW! Do not wait until you have enough money or life is more comfortable or the timing is more convenient or it somehow feels right. *Act now!*

If God grants you another day, then take another action on that one item or begin to work your way down your list. Tell people you love how special they are. Begin to repair broken relationships. Pick up the phone now and make a start. Take the first step. *Now!*

CHAPTER 10

The distance from being <u>broke</u> to being rich *is measured in inches*. The distance from being <u>poor</u> to being rich *is measured in miles*.

Rags to Riches . . .
Applying the Philosophy

Many thousands of people who have taken our corporate, public, and network marketing workshops have produced tangible, incredible results. They have saved their marriages, lost weight, quit smoking, changed jobs, found satisfying work, increased their incomes, and fulfilled many different dreams.

I want to share with you just one of many stories of people who have applied the philosophy contained in this book and used it to pursue their dreams. This is Alan Nagao's story, a man who literally started with nothing and rose to great heights. He is a bright beacon of hope and inspiration to all those who think they have too much stacked against them to succeed.

Even if Alan's good fortune should take a turn for the worse in the future, he will recreate his fortune once again by applying the same philosophy. That "can do" belief system is part of his secret. Alan is not afraid to lose. He knows he can overcome again and again. If Alan can do it, so can you!

Alan was awarded K&A's first annual Product of the Philosophy Award.

Alan Nagao

Alan was a twenty-four-year-old student in a seminar I taught back in 1988. Born in Hawaii and not an academic standout in high school, Alan chose not to go on to college. He was not the most popular young man and was not particularly athletic. In fact, he was born without a leg and has a deformed hand.

Four years before attending the seminar, Alan started his own company, High Performance Kites, which later became HPK Marketing. When we first met, Alan was earning about $600 a month selling kites.

To earn $60 in one day was a big deal for him, but Alan had set a goal: owning a store in the Ala Moana Mall, a major shopping mall in Honolulu. It was a prestigious site and application acceptance for a storefront was difficult to obtain. He had no track record or financial history and was turned down twice before management finally approved his application. (Persistence should be his middle name!)

Over time, Alan wanted to expand his kite business. He decided to create a yo-yo boom in Hawaii. Now, the state of Hawaii only has one million people and a yo-yo is obviously not what most people would consider a necessity. Yo-yos were not even popular at the time. However, faithfully using the visualization techniques discussed in this book, Alan fashioned a yo-yo marketing plan that turned yo-yos into a must-have product. Alan created a genuine yo-yo boom in Hawaii, selling more yo-yos in Hawaii than were sold in the rest of the United States!

Alan then decided to expand once again, this time to Japan. However, he had no contacts in Japan, he did not speak the language, and a much-needed manufacturer of yo-yos was not returning his phone calls or faxes. His finances were also running low and his wife, Priscilla, unknown to Alan, had pulled money out of their life insurance policy to finance a final trip to the reluctant manufacturer.

Undeterred, Alan set a goal to sell one million yo-yos in Japan. A long story short, Alan's company sold over ten million yo-yos in Japan, creating the world's largest yo-yo boom ever! Ten years after meeting Alan, his company sales were $13 million, a far cry from $600 per month!

What parts of the philosophy did Alan apply that you can apply too? I wanted to find out as well, so I interviewed Alan in 1999. (That interview is now part of our Mastery of Money tape series available at www.klemmer.com.)

The rest of Alan's story

During the pursuit of his dream, Alan met and married a wonderful woman named Priscilla, and they now have two beautiful children. They have a solid relationship and are wonderful people to be around. They are also active in the community and in humanitarian organizations. As President of the YMCA of Hawaii, Alan volunteers a great deal of time in his community, believing that as we give, so shall we receive.

As Alan's company grew, he decided to take seven months off to build a house with his father, fulfilling a desire to deepen their relationship. In short, Alan is an example of a balanced square. In contrast, how many people do you know who are so busy chasing their success that they complain there is never enough time for anything else?

None of this is to say that Alan is perfect. He makes mistakes, just like anyone else. In fact, he plans on it! One of his mottos is: "To up your success rate, up your willingness to fail." He believes that half of his marketing ideas will fail and he has created a system for minimizing failure. His system includes simple things like test-marketing an idea in a small market where he can limit the downside and leveraging his test-marketed success in a larger market.

Alan and Priscilla started with nothing and yet they have created a balanced life, a life that includes a full family life, financial success, contribution to others, and a belief in God. If they can do it, so can you. Why not? I cannot think of a good reason why not. Can you?

If you can, remove those sunglasses. Toss out those old tapes. Rip up that tattered map. Take that heavy sack of manure off your back. Toss that pumpkin on your head off the mountain. There are dreams to pursue!

Alan's philosophy

In the 1999 interview, I asked Alan what aspects of the philosophy he found most applicable to his success. Here are the ten key points he shared with me that day:

1. **Write down your goals.** Alan is a fanatic in this area. He has a written goal statement on his desk and in his car and he says it aloud, like an affirmation, several times a day.

2. **Continue to learn and grow**. Alan took three years to learn, apply, and perfect the visualization technique we cover in our seminars. He also went to other seminars, hired a success tutor, and continues to grow in his business and personal goals.

3. **Be persistent.** Alan continued to send faxes to a manufacturer after they rejected his proposal and he repeatedly asked for space in Ala Moana shopping mall after being turned down. He focuses on what he wants and he continues to persevere.

4. **Play the game for maximum gain**. Most people play life in order not to lose rather than for maximum gain. Alan could have rested after his success in Hawaii, but he was willing to incur risks in order to expand into Japan. Again, he could have rested after his success in Japan, but he expanded into six new countries and grew from seven employees to over sixty. Alan was willing to take risks to achieve maximum gain.

5. **Establish good habits.** In his business, Alan sets up systems to insure successful habits for giving, risking, handling failure, communication, and learning.

6. **Have a strong belief in God.** Alan purposely takes on challenges he knows he cannot do in his own strength as a way of forcing his subconscious, and inviting his God, to come to his aid.

7. **Live a balanced life.** As well as working on his business, Alan spends time working on his relationships, health, spirituality, and community.

8. **Be a giver.** In 1998, Alan gave away $120,000 of his own money. Even when he had very little, he practiced this principle. When he only earned $600 a month, he gave away $60 a month. Alan provides his employees with company-paid time off so they can give to the community.

9. **Practice visualization to creatively solve problems.** Whether it is developing a way to create a boom for yo-yos or deciding on what opportunity to pursue next, Alan uses visualization to go beyond what reason and logic alone can produce.

10. **Develop a *Win-Win* attitude.** Alan believes in the *Win-Win* approach. Whether it is between two employees or between his company HPK and a manufacturer, he truly wants to see everyone work together and mutually benefit.

Dare to dream

My mentor always told me, "I am nobody special. Whatever I have done, anybody can do . . . if they are willing to pay the price and apply the philosophy."

If you are willing to pay the price and apply the philosophy, you too can achieve your dreams, just as Alan fulfilled his.

Many people, like the baby boomers of my generation, spend too much time and energy trying to "find themselves." Let Alan's story and this book be the end of trying to find your self. *Let this be the beginning of creating yourself and your dream!* Let it lead you to finding and winning with others. Let it help you create your own life story.

Dare to dream your impossible dream.

Dare to climb that mountain.

Dare to break old habits.

Dare to have a vision and purpose.

Dare to pursue it every day, as if it were your first day and your last day on earth.

You can do it! Do it now!

Epilogue

The ability to create the experience you want, regardless of your circumstances, is called *mastery*. Most people believe they can only be successful if their circumstances are perfectly aligned and positive, but rarely do circumstances line up as we desire or expect either in our business or personal life.

This book is your guide to becoming a master of life, a person who achieves results based on their faithfulness to a specific philosophy, a philosophy that achieves results no matter what your immediate circumstances.

Liberty is the result of mastery. Liberty is:

- **the ability to do what you want to do, when you want to do it, not just when someone with authority says you can or cannot do it.**

- **the ability to go where you want to go, when you want to go, not just when someone else says you can.**

- **the ability to become what you want to be within the time frame you set for it to happen.**

- **the ability to create what you want for your life and to create it *now*.**

Mastery has very little to do with intelligence. In fact, you probably know some highly educated people who are unemployed or who have experienced failed relationships. But with mastery, if you want financial independence, you can create it, and create it quickly.

Mastery is proactive. It encompasses more than the understanding of a set philosophy; it is the *practice* of that philosophy that leads to desired results. It is not only destination oriented, but also process oriented. It matters how you arrive, not just that you arrive! Mastery is a combination of awareness and skills working in harmony.

Most successful people acknowledge God or a higher being. I believe it is God's plan and desire to prosper you in every area of your life. If you are not prospering, it is not His fault. You are simply not playing the game of life as it was designed. You must learn to master the game of life.

I have a belief, and like all beliefs, it may or may not be true. As a Christian, I find a verse in the Bible confirming of God's desire: "I pray that you may prosper in all things and be in health, just as your soul prospers" (3 John 1:2). In all of our natures—physical, mental, emotional, and spiritual—we are to experience abundance.

If you are not a Christian, but belong to another faith, look through your Holy Book for a similar teaching. I believe that you will find, whatever you call God, that He wants you to prosper. If you have no belief in God, then my prayer is that this book will open the door for you to discover a greater being or a higher consciousness than yourself.

I caution you, however, that the road to mastery will not be easy just because you believe in God. Masters of Life still have big challenges, *but they are better prepared to meet them.* Belief in God transcends this world and is a huge advantage when it comes to playing the game of life.

One of my dear friends, Jay Golby, once said, "Let me see your check book and I will tell you what is important to you."

How true! What we spend our time and money on speaks volumes about what we value. If you spend time and money on your family, it tells me they are important to you. If you spend time and money on seeking God and doing His work, that tells me He is important to you. If you spend time and money on books, tapes, and seminars to educate yourself, to become a master of life—one who is able to produce or create results—that tells me that mastery is important to you.

The fairest way to gauge anything is by results. Often harsh, always fair. Your wishing or wanting will not create mastery. Only a *true intention* will, as shown by action.

Only you can decide whether you want to live life as an eagle or as an oyster. Certainly, it may be more dangerous and more difficult to be an eagle than an oyster, but it is far more rewarding. The oyster lives in a sheltered environment, "safe" but stuck, dependent on the leftovers of other animals. The eagle enjoys the freedom of the skies. It has tremendous vision. It knows what it wants and needs and it persists until it succeeds. It masters the skies!

If you choose to be an eagle, someone who applies the philosophy of this book, then you will put a plan into *ACTION*. Nothing happens when you merely observe. Masters acknowledge that continued growth and learning is an ongoing part of life. Are you willing to spend the necessary time studying and mastering the material in this book? Are you willing to practice hard to become a master? Or would you rather be known as someone who only knows *about* the game rather than knowing how to play the game?

For instance, can you develop strong, toned muscles by watching me lift weights or by talking about lifting weights? Of course not! You might be impressed by my ability to lift weights and even learn a great deal about weight lifting, but watching me does nothing for your muscles. You have to get involved. You have to lift your own weights. You have to practice your own commitment.

Continuing your journey: *TWO NEXT STEPS*

Next step #1: Using this book as a Master of Life Manual, I suggest you take one chapter each week and read that chapter every day for seven days. Consciously and proactively apply the ideas of the chapter you are reading to at least one situation in your life. Practice the concept. Set aside time to do this.

At the end of the week, move on to the next chapter. Read that chapter every day for a week. It will take you approximately twenty minutes a day to do the reading and a little more time to do the required exercises in order to apply the ideas. It will take ten weeks to complete the entire book in this fashion.

Will you commit to continuing your journey in this fashion? The eagle in you is calling!

> **NOTE:** If you complete this ten-week reading of the entire book, send us your name and address and any of your wins and successes. Enclose $3.50 for shipping and handling and we will send you two tapes valued at $25. The first tape is a great interview with George Leonard, inventor of the Samurai game that we use in our **Advanced Leadership Seminar**. The

second tape is by myself and is about overcoming obstacles. It outlines seven keys to overcoming obstacles on your journey toward mastery. These two gifts are our way of saying, "Congratulations on changing your life!"

Next step #2: You can attend a two-and-a-half-hour evening **Champions Workshop**[2] in your area for free (valued at $59!), by mailing in the perforated postcard in the back. This night will be a monumental step in your life journey!

Now, take a moment to look at the lists below. You can see the great need for leadership that exists in the United States and around the world.

The need for leadership in the United States:

- One in two children live in a single parent family at some point in their childhood

- One in three five-to-seventeen-year-olds are behind a year or more in school

- One in four is born to a mother who did not graduate from high school

- One in seven have no health insurance

- One in eight drop out of school

- One in nine are born into a family living at less than half the poverty level

- One in twelve have a disability

- One in twenty-five report being abused or neglected in any given year

- One in 120 die before their first birthday

- One in 610 will be killed by a gun before their twentieth birthday

- One in five live in a family that receives food stamps

- One in three are born to an unmarried parent

The need for leadership in the world

- 50 percent of people in the world do not have clean sanitation water

- 20 percent do not have adequate shelter

- 33 percent go to bed hungry each night

- 3 percent die of hunger every year

- 70 percent are unable to read

- Only 1 percent are college educated

It does not have to be this way. The need for mastery is urgent. As you fulfill your own dreams, you make a difference in the world around you. When you become a master of life, you have the power to affect the lives of others in unimaginable ways!

Will you do it? Will you make a commitment to get your life in shape? Will you make an agreement to follow the plan for the next ninety days? The eagle in you is calling. Your dreams are calling. Start the exciting journey right now!

---

[2] See page 160 for more information

Recommended Reading

Choose any twelve of these excellent books and read one a month for one year:

Mastery, by George Leonard

Rich Dad, Poor Dad, by Robert Kiyosaki

Body for Life, by Bill Phillips

Mach 2, With Your Hair on Fire, by Richard Brooke

Magic of Conflict, by Tom Crumm

Riches Within Your Reach, by Robert Collier

Operating Manual for Spaceship Earth, by R. Buckminister Fuller

The Business of Discovering the Future, by Joel Barker

Think & Grow Rich, by Napoleon Hill

100th Monkey, by Ken Keyes, Jr.

The Game of Life & How to Play It, by Florence Scovel Shinn

7 Habits of Highly Effective People, by Steven Covey

Sacred Hoops, by Phil Jackson

I Dare You, by William Danforth

Psychocybernetics, by Dr. Maxwell Maltz

Winning Through Enlightenment, by Ron Smotherman

Diet for a New America, by John Robbins

Bible, or your own religious book

Our Mission . . .

*Creating bold ethical leaders who will create a world
that works for everyone with no one left out.*

The Klemmer & Associates "PhD" in Leadership
Development

1—Champions Workshop: A one-evening interactive
exploration of "the Formula of Champions" as an intro-
duction to the Klemmer & Associates Leadership
Seminars. Learn how to produce results when you have
no idea what to do.

2—Personal Mastery: A weekend seminar in awareness
where you explore the belief systems that make most of
your decisions and prevent the success you say you want.

3—Advanced Leadership Seminar: A five-day breakthrough experience in leadership. Discover within you
the attributes of a compassionate Samurai; one who is
bold, focused, personally responsible, committed, honest,
with the attitude of abundance and service to others.

4—Heart of the Samurai Seminar: This six-day experience in leveraging your personal results and service to
the world will generate an extraordinary level of abundance; financially, spiritually, mentally, and emotionally.
Come prepared to have a fun time with graduates from
all over the world.

5—Samurai Camp: This is a sixty-day program to establish the habits and practices of a Samurai for a life of
significance and success on your terms.

To reach Brian Klemmer or Klemmer & Associates:

BY PHONE:
(415) 506-0300

TOLL FREE:
(800) 577-5447

BY FAX:
(415) 382-3477

BY U.S. MAIL:
24 Digital Drive, Suite #1
Novato, CA 94949

By E-mail:
mastery@klemmer.com

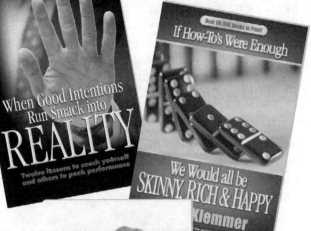

Champions Workshop

The Champions Workshop is a 2-½ hour fun, impacting, and experiential workshop based on the "Formula of Champions." Brian Klemmer has interviewed Olympic world record holding athletes, CEOs of major corporations, and successful people of all walks of life in an effort to find the common denominators and keys to success. *The Formula of Champions is the result!*

Have you ever wanted something but were stuck because you didn't know what to do? *Never again! Here is a formula for producing results when you have no idea what to do. You can put this to use immediately.*

Is there a gap between what you want and what you actually get? *Learn why what you want has nothing to do with what you create.*

Mail in the attached perforated postcard and you can attend for FREE! This power-packed, riveting workshop is one of many workshops offered by Klemmer & Associates worldwide. Regularly $59!

If you need further information, call 800-577-5477 or visit <u>www.klemmer.com</u>.